BROTHER
AGAINST
BROTHER

"There comes a time when silence is betrayal"
Martin Luther King, Jr.

BROTHER AGAINST BROTHER

AMERICA'S NEW WAR OVER LAND RIGHTS

DIANA WHITE HORSE CAPP

The Free Enterprise Press
BELLEVUE, WASHINGTON
Distributed by Merril Press

First Edition
Published by the Free Enterprise Press

Typeset in Times New Roman by The Free Enterprise Press, a division of
the Center for the Defense of Free Enterprise, 12500 N.E. 10th Place,
Bellevue, Washington 98005. Telephone 425-455-5038. Fax 425-451-
3959. E-mail address: books@cdfe.org. Cover design by Northwoods
Studio.

BROTHER **AGAINST** BROTHER is distributed by Merril Press,
P.O. Box 1682, Bellevue, Washington 98009. Additional copies of
this book may be ordered from Merril Press at $15.00 each. Phone
425-454-7009.

LIBRARY OF CONGRESS CATALOGING-IN-PUBLICATION DATA
Capp, Diana White Horse, 1952-
    Brother against brother : America's new war over land rights /
Diana White Horse Capp.
        p.   cm.
    Includes bibliographical references and index.
    ISBN 0-939571-22-6 (pbk.)
    1. Indians of North America--Land tenure. 2. Right of property--
United States. 3. Environmentalism--United States. 4. Eminent
domain--United States. I. Title.

E93 .C32 2002
323.4'6'08997073--dc21

                                                2002029663

CONTENTS

Dedication

With thanks
for my parents' belief in human rights,
our ancestors' will to survive,
and the incentive to persist
that my children provide—

This book is dedicated to them,
to all the peoples of the land who have struggled
for their dignity throughout time,
and to a brighter future for all the children.

Preface

My father, you have made promises to me and to my children.
If the promises had been made by a person of no standing, I should not be surprised to see his promises fail.
But you, who are so great in riches and power; I am astonished that I do not see your promises fulfilled! I would have been better pleased if you had never made such promises than that you should have made them and not performed them.

Shinguaconse - "Little Pine"

In the interest of justice, I offer this book to Indian and non-Indian communities across the American landscape. As we enter the 21st century, an urgent need to correct a bewildering tangle of injustices old and new is upon us. Only then will America really portray its ideals of freedom and human dignity.

Many of these injustices occur in rural America. They threaten the social and economic well-being of land-based communities, and damage the overall unity of the nation.

The view I present of these injustices may seem a bit unusual. Yet they say it is the 'mixed bloods' who will build a bridge between America's first peoples and those who arrived after Columbus. My own family history is one of cultural oppression and repeated government taking of our lands. With these experiences and their lessons in mind, I hope to contribute to the integrity of that bridge.

I do not speak for anyone's opinion but my own. I do, however, speak in urgent support of the human rights and freedoms we must have to reject plutocracy and promote human dignity. These are the same rights and freedoms the new American union began to embrace when it adopted the principles of the Iroquois Constitution for its own.

Central to these human rights and freedoms is this: All rural land-based peoples must be able to exercise control over the lands upon which they live and toil. This aspect of sovereignty is necessary to guarantee their socioeconomic security. Ultimately, only that can guarantee the security of the entire American people.

Any other arrangement leads to the abuse and impoverishment of land-based communities. Indigenous activist Winona LaDuke points this out in her 1998 interview with David Barsamian. "Indian people are poor because of structural poverty. Structural poverty means you don't actually control your land, your economy.....You control your land and you control your economy."

Only when we apply this freedom to all will we finally break the old chains of slavery and offer the truest seeds of hope to humanity.

Before we can achieve this worthy goal, we must resolve the conflicting claims to land and water that government policy and action create.

I submit this suggestion to the American people: If we can not rely on government to uphold the promises it makes in Indian treaties, then we can not rely on government to honor land grants, land patents, property rights, water rights and all the other promises it makes. Many of these government promises overlap, create racial conflict, and harm rural communities. Together, we *should* demand government accountability for its conflicting promises and the harm they do. We must be proactive. We must come together to resolve these conflicts. This course of action seems far more logical and constructive than fighting each other.

Today we find that laws intended to protect our environment often result in new claims for land and water. These new claims make the conflicts that government's overlapping promises create even more complicated. Again, we must hold government accountable. We must demand that laws made to protect our environment actually work. We must reward good stewardship rather than simply punish offenders. We must also demand that these laws do not diminish local control or harm the rural land-based communities involved.

Conflicting government promises for land and water unfairly places the American people in a fight against each other. They do not just fight for government's promises to them. They fight for their very social and economic survival. This fight echoes the pain caused by the Indian Wars and the Civil War—it pits brother against brother. This is America's new war over land rights. Government's broken promises create this war. It is a war we must honorably resolve.

Many people helped in writing this book. For inspiration and un-flagging belief in me and my message I owe most to Anne Novakovitch. For his willingness to accept my manuscript for publication, I am grateful to Free Enterprise Press publisher Alan Gottlieb. To Free Enterprise Press editor in chief Ron Arnold, my thanks for suggestions and guidance through the intricacies of the publishing world. A big "thank you" to Sandy Fields for keeping good records and hard work on the final page proofs. If this book has merit, I attribute it to the dedication of these fine people. Any errors of fact or judgment are mine alone.

Brother Against Brother—America's New War Over Land Rights follows my own journey of land dispossession. It explores the causes and searches out solutions for our land and water conflicts. It seeks a just and honorable end to America's new war over land rights.

Part One

The War
That Never Really Ended

They made us many promises, more than I can remember.
They never kept but one -
They promised to take our land, and they took it.

--Red Cloud, Oglala Lakota

- Chapter One -

The Trail That Never Ends

Wrapped in the muggy blanket of Appalachian summer and the timeless comfort of clannish laughter, we rolled along in our auto-mobiles. Our destination was a place most people call Indiantown Gap. Back then, I was just a little tangle-hair girl in a meandering parade of relations packed into old Packards, Ramblers, Chevys and Hudsons. We were loaded from headliners to floorboards with playful country kids and homemade picnic fixings.

The whole Capp clan was hitting the trail for one glorious day in our old homeland in the Blue Mountains. It was a pilgrimage of secret Indians. We were just a fragment of many others like us who remained in Pennsylvania, silenced and forgotten. Indiantown Gap was still dotted with Lenape farms and villages not nearly so long ago as official histories say. The Blue Mountains, some say, were the last stronghold. Like beauty, history itself is also in the eye of the beholder.

Indiantown Gap is the name derived from the general area around Manada Gap to Swatara Gap, and the people who lived there. Both gaps are notches in the first of the Blue Mountains. Both open north into a wide valley and the Second Mountain. The Capps lived along the upper reaches of Manada Creek, and what my elders fondly remembered as Fishing Creek Valley.

Surely the Blue Mountains are the most beautiful place on Earth! Our visits seemed almost like a waking dream. It was as though we were on a one day pass to an earlier time when our ancestors could join us for the feast we carried.

The grown-ups lounged on picnic blankets spread across the earth like a giant crazy quilt. Drinking in the Valley - as they called it - they remembered the old days. They took such obvious pleasure in us wild little children as we ran circles around them. Soft green light poured through the great tent of Eastern woodland foliage. Squealing cousins splashed and ran through the creek as though the copperheads and rattlesnakes our aunties warned us of did not exist.

All day our noisy pack of cousins swarmed around the Valley. Toward the end of that day, we wondered—why did we *ever* leave this place? It was a perplexing mystery to us children.

Another mystery was the shattered old foundation in which our grown-up relations took such interest. It was whispered among us children that it used to be our home. Yet it looked more like a gruesome tomb than the remains of a family farmhouse. How did it come to be in this awful condition? It surely seemed like the adults hovered over this grim-looking spot the way mourners peer into a loved one's open grave. We got no explanation from them.

On the return trip, our caravan would also visit the little old grave-yard at Moonshine Church. It is located near Saint Joseph Springs, not too far from our old home in the Valley. The cemetery was shrouded in a tale the grown-ups knew all about—the murdering Blue Eyed Six and ghostly blue eyes that hover over their graves at night. Their victim, too, is buried here.

Other people said that troubled Indian spirits also linger there. The whole matter seemed very meaningful to the grown-ups. Yet, they would tell me only that the Blue Eyed Six were real mean people who murdered 'a man'. That's all I needed to know, they said—just be quiet and watch-out for mean people like the Blue Eyed Six.

The grown-ups were usually so open and kind. It frustrated me when they clammed-up like that. This business of the Blue Eyed Six aggravated my curiosity. But more than anything else, I wanted to know why we had moved away from the Valley.

Yet, they were all uniquely deaf to questions of why we left the home they so plainly loved. It was clear that decades later they continued to mourn. Not a child easily deterred, I pondered the mystery endlessly. I hunted any chance to catch an unwary relative off guard, stalking the hidden answers.

Mother's lips were sealed tight. Also silent, were my great aunts, Joyce, Nanny and Auntie Kate. Grandma Lillian was the oldest of the women now, and reminded me a great stout crow. Her cozy lap was the throne of my comfort and security. Yet she was not to be charmed, not even by her eldest granddaughter, into divulging any secret before its appointed time.

Then one summer day Great Uncle John, the traveling man, caught me by surprise. I was dallying alone in the yard. He was back home from his adventures for a spell and came looking for his inquisitive little grand niece. His willingness to indulge the usual barrage of questions pleased me no end. Even so, he would not explain the big secret. Instead he pressed a coin, a quarter, into my hand. "For your birthday," he told me.

I was happy, but confused. It wasn't my birthday. I looked up at him uncertainly. Uncle made an urgent nod toward the coin. "Look, Tiana. It has an eagle on it." He positioned the eagle just right in the palm of my little hand. "Look at the eagle, Tiana. Look at it," he urged.

I studied the raised image the quarter bore, rubbed my thumb over its wings. Uncle's voice became intent. His words were measured and somber. "Tiana, you must go to Washington state when you grow up. Go to Puget Sound. They still keep the Indian way. You will find the eagle there."

I looked up into Uncle's face, his eyes like dark stars. "Tiana," he commanded, "Never forget who you are." Uncle departed as quickly as he had appeared. There would be no more questions.

Back in the 1950s it was still illegal for Indian people to practice their own religious traditions. Perhaps that's why Grandma called such things her 'superstitions'.

As a young child, Uncle John's words were surprising to me. I wasn't sure there *were* other Indians left. The only ones I knew existed were my own secretive, self-isolated relatives. Most of them refused to speak of their Indian identity in front of strangers. The men were more forthright, but a couple of the women refused to even speak of it to us children. My little cousins and I did not understand this secretive behavior. It frustrated me, it angered me…it grieved me.

The schoolteachers talked as though Indian people were all long gone. Somehow history went from pilgrims and Indians having a merry feast at the first Thanksgiving, and William Penn's treaty with the Lenape, right straight to the teachers' version of modern day Pennsylvania. It made me feel like a ghost. I wanted to holler out, 'You lie! We are right here!' Outside the school building doors I did holler it out…and got in fights about it with other children.

Voltaire once said that William Penn's treaty with the Lenape was "the one treaty with the Indians that the whites never broke." But that is not true. William kept the treaty, but his sons had a way of stretching boundaries, and cheated scandalously on a fraudulent document called the Walking Purchase after their father died.

Charles II granted Pennsylvania to a Quaker religious dissenter named William Penn, in 1682. Penn had been kicked out of Oxford University and arrested for his unpopular religious beliefs. Yet his wealthy father's estate was owed money by the Crown. Unusual for his time, William Penn believed that his land grant from the English king did not extinguish Indian rights to the land. He believed that he must first purchase the land from the Indian people. Only then could he begin his colony of religious tolerance, his "Holy Experiment" in the land that came to be called Pennsylvania, meaning Penn's Woods.

Penn sent William Markham to negotiate his purchase of southeast Pennsylvania from the Lenape. Penn arrived afterward to sign the treaty at Shackamaxon, now called Philadelphia, with Tammamend, a local sachem, or chief, not that of the entire Lenape Nation. Because the land west of the Lenape was then occupied by the Susquehannocks, Penn went back to England with no western boundary established for this purchase. Upon his return in 1699, he discovered that the Iroquois League of nations required the Susquehannocks and Lenape to gain the league's permission before selling land. When the Iroquois League found out about the treaty Tammamend signed, trouble arose between them and the Lenape.

By the time of Penn's death in 1718, the Iroquois Confederacy had authority over Lenape affairs. The English governors of Pennsylvania supported this because they wanted to make sure the Lenape did not ally with the French against them. Many Lenape had migrated west and north to the upper valleys of the rivers that flowed from east from the Blue Mountains because of the English presence. The military alliance called the "covenant chain" eventually proved little protection because the majority of the Lenape warriors were lost in wars the Iroquois League was fighting on other fronts. In 1722, the Tuscarora, but not the Lenape, were given full membership in the League. With their western treaty boundaries still unclear, the Lenape continued to be pushed west.

When Penn died his three sons inherited his estate. However, his sons and other agents had been selling land to pay their creditors, lands which were still owned by the Lenape. In 1737, Pennsylvania officials suddenly claimed they found a fifty-one year old 1686 treaty. The Penns fraudulently claimed an old, incomplete, unsigned draft of a deed was actually a legal contract to cede land, the supposed signers long dead. The Lenape had to reluctantly agree to the fraudulent document. The Penn's claimed the tribe signed away all the land between the convergence of the Delaware and Lehigh Rivers for as far west as a man could walk in a day and a half.

As if the questionable authenticity of this treaty wasn't bad enough, even this wasn't enough land to please Penn's sons. Thomas Penn hired three of the fastest runners in Pennsylvania to establish the boundary of the infamous Walking Purchase. He arranged for the runners to follow a path already cleared of obstacles for them, with horseback riders supplying them with drink of rum, sugar and lime for their run. The one who ran the furthest was to receive a valuable prize. The walking distance should have been about forty miles. But the winner ran twice the distance the Lenape were led to expect. 1200 square miles of Pennsylvania, an area about the size of Rhode Island, was thus ceded. This is how the Penn's cheated to get most of the Lehigh River Valley.

The Lenape expected the League to help defend them against this whole fraud. But now they were very angry because they believed the Lenape had signed another treaty without League permission. Those living in the Lehigh Valley had little choice but to join the other Lenape living in the upper Susquehanna regions. The former Susquehannock territory then served as reservations for the Lenape and other peoples being pushed out.

Those camps were crowded, sometimes very unhealthy. A number of tribal groups including Lenape, Shawnee, remnants of New England area tribes, Seneca, Mingo and Cayuga camped in the Valley. All were under the supervision of Shikellamy, the Vice-Regent appointed by the Iroquois Confederacy. Captain John Logan, one of his four sons, replaced Shikellamy after his death. James Logan eventually became widely known as Chief Logan of the Mingo.

In the mid 1700's my ancestors camped in that area, from Shamokin south to Whiconescong, now called Wiconisco. Tusannah, or Emma Logan (Capp), remained behind with Jacob Capp and the villages that remained when the camps once again moved on in the Eastern tribes' seemingly endless migration. The Lenape eventually signed 18 treaties. But, many Lenape found ways to remain in the East, quietly sticking like burrs in the folds of the Appalachians and isolated spots throughout the original territory. Many small villages were strung along the Blue Mountains.

The Lenape people were called the "grandfathers" by many Indian nations, with many tribal groups springing from this ancient people. From 1632 on, they had also taken in many Algonquin refugees from among the Powhattan, Munsee, Wappinger, Wicomiss, Assateague, New England Algonquin, Shawnee, Conoy, Saponi, Tutelo, Nanticoke and Mahican. Yet in the end, the Lenape were not treated with respect. Though many remained in eastern Pennsylvania, most were forced to move on through western Pennsylvania, Ohio, Kansas, Oklahoma, Texas, and even Idaho.

Many of the Lenape who moved on now have state or federal recognition. Yet the state of Pennsylvania refuses to recognize the Lenape people who never left. Those who oppose recognition focus the public's fears on Indian gaming that is legal if a tribe is federally recognized.

However, the state already has the lottery and race track betting. Perhaps some are really more concerned about possible land claims. So, the truth of continual Lenape presence in the state is still officially denied.

The old time Big Houses, the focus of spiritual life in the East, had been torched and destroyed many years before I came along. In the old days, the Quakers tried to protect the Lenape from anti-Indian colonists, and did not try to convert them. But the Moravians, actually rather cruel masters who sometimes even sold Lenape people, tried to claim our souls. Yet many of the converted were still murdered by the vigilante Paxtang Boys. Later the United Brethren branched from the Moravian Church, taking Lenape into their churches.

Pretty soon, keeping the old religion was dangerous, something to be done deep in the forest, or at least far from the eyes of condemnation and punishment, if at all. Being Indian was risky business. Children were shielded from knowledge that could get their people killed. This is how the Lenape people in the East survived over the generations.

But Great Uncle John knew of people far away on Puget Sound who had continued on with their winter ceremonial dances in the Big House despite the law. John roamed the nation like a scout. The rails were his pony. Yet twenty some years passed after he placed that quarter into my little hand, before I learned the full reason for his restlessness.

Back in childhood, there were so many things I did not know. I might have asked Great Uncle Charles why we left Indiantown Gap, but he rarely spoke as far as I could tell. He read a lot, but spoke little. He was wounded in the War. Shrapnel.

Still, I persisted, looking for that perfect moment. Riding along on
the tractor's fender. Maybe while shucking corn. Dressing chickens, tossing horseshoes, picking berries. But the grown-ups
guarded their secret as though it would surely bite me like a mean
old snake if I were to know.

Great Uncle Levi was a patient, good-natured man. I pestered
him about Indiantown Gap endlessly. I tried to take a subtle approach, shadowing him around the farm for hours and then -
suddenly - I'd spring my question on him in a roundabout way.
"Uncle, where did we come from?"

But there was no fooling him. "You come from right here, Tiana.
We live right here," he'd tease. "*Before* that, Uncle," I'd press
him. "You been there," he'd say. And then I'd say it— "But
how'd we get *here*, Uncle?" "From south of here," was his cryp-
tic reply, referring to the old migration. If I came right out and
asked *why* we left the Valley, he would go into his rendition of
"Way Down Yonder in the Indian Nations". Then he would go
right on with whatever he had been doing.

So I would sulk and shut up about it for a while. This secret gave
me no end of frustration.

Great Grandpa Jake had *somehow* moved the family to the farm
where I grew up sometime after we left Indiantown, back in 1932.
That was twenty years before I came along to worry them all
with questions.

This new farm was about seventeen miles away from Indiantown
Gap. Now we were in the rolling Appalachian foothills that
sprouted Lenape arrowheads every time we plowed. A tiny nation of our own, four generations of Capp's lived together there in
one, and then in time, several houses.

We children had no end of fun jumping through hay holes in the
barn, swinging like jungle warriors on thick vines that dangled from
the trees in the cool, damp shadows of the pasture's wooded creek
valley. Summer evenings we gathered with the grown-ups set
upon their chairs between great pillar-like trees in the front yard.

We never tired of the theater show sure to unfold before us. As if on cue, the white tail deer would slowly glide across the facing hill from one stand of forest to the other, accompanied by musical frogs, symphonic crickets and vast constellations of flashing lightning bugs.

When the show was over, we kids often played our boogie man game. We dared in the dark night to creep toward a shadowed out building that concealed our appointed boogie man. Within he waited silently, hidden among the saddles and summer kitchen gear. Then suddenly he jumped out and roared like a maniac, chasing the laughing, shrieking children. If he caught you, you had to be boogie man, and hide yourself somewhere to terrorize the cousins.

On this land we could be archers and sharpshooters, hut builders and horse riders. In winter, massive hard-packed snowdrifts were hollowed out to render cozy snow caves. The great hills in which the farm was tucked provided sledding beyond compare. When the deep snows came it would take days to free the driveways to connection with the outside world again.

We all grew up swaddled in a land of wild woods and thickets, fertile fields and watchful relatives. We knew and loved every inch of that farm as though it was our mother. Little did us children realize that our farm was being ever so slowly devoured by a new zoning scheme. It all began with taxing the land on which we grew food as though it were residential, like suburbia. Our childhood ignorance was a sort of bliss that now seems quite shortlived.

I now understand they called it 'agricultural-residential zoning'. It is a practice of those who want to force unwilling country folks to sell their land. These are the sort of people who think they have a better use for your land than you do. These people believe they are significantly more intelligent, and therefore more deserving of your land. What it means for farmers is that they have to sell off land to satisfy inflated property taxes every year until there is no farm left.

Urbanized humans do not, perhaps cannot, fathom that people of the land love the land from which their generations grew. We love it with such depth, such affection, that it actually causes physical pain and heartbreak to be separated from it.

To us, our land is not just some interchangeable piece of real estate. It is not recreational property, nor a nature retreat to recreate the frazzled civilized soul. The land certainly is not an object of flowery philosophical fantasy devoid of humans like the advocates of 'wilderness values' rattle on about. The land the Creator has allowed our successive generations to intertwine with is part of our very heart and soul.

My dad's maternal relatives appeared suspiciously like my mother's people, but they had come to live in the city of Lebanon. Grandma Daubert seemed to know way too much about the Blue Mountain and its people.

My dad's father, however, was quite different from either family. He was from a Pennsylvania German farm in the Suedberg area, also along the Blue Mountains. The Daubert farm was just a bit north of Indiantown Gap.

Grandpa Joe was big as a barn, with curly blonde hair, blue eyes, and a speaking voice that might as well have been thunder. Grandpa had gotten into the plumbing and heating business after he married Grandma and moved away from his own family. They say he single-handedly carried claw-foot cast-iron tubs up staircases on his back.

As a child, I thought Joe Daubert was the biggest man in the world. He never uttered an unkind word to me. Yet, I was not tempted to fluster him with endless questions, especially while he was fishing or watching football. Perhaps I'd heard too many references to the Blue Eyed Six.

It was back in 1878 that the six blue eyed men took out 'graveyard insurance' on Joseph Raber. Raber lived alone in a little charcoal burner's shack in Saint Joseph's Springs, an old Lenape village site. The six men made themselves the insurance beneficiaries. Back then you could take out such a policy on a person you weren't even related to. That was certainly the case with Mr. Raber and the blue eyed six. They murdered poor Mr. Raber for the insurance money.

Because the Capp grown-ups only alluded mysteriously to this event around us children, we only knew that we had better watch out for mean people like the Blue Eyed Six. Unfortunately, we didn't know who they were. So, when I was a little kid, this grim warning about people like the blue eyed six made me scared of people with blue eyes. Poor old Grandpa Joe, he had nothing to do with those murderers. Now I wish I had just pestered the daylights out of him. He really was a friendly, jovial man.

Grandpa Joe's people still spoke Pennsylvania German among themselves. Their farm was along the Swatara Creek. Oh, that, too, was a beautiful place.

Daddy said that Grandpa Daubert's first ancestor here in America, a farmer, served as a bodyguard for General Washington in the Revolutionary War. Enlisted farmers went home to plant in the spring, he said, left to fight during summer, returned home to harvest in fall, and went back to war for the winter. That way both the people and the revolutionary army continued to be fed.

That is what made it so shocking when we got the big news, because Grandpa Joe wasn't Indian. He was a white descendant of the American Revolution. It was a Sunday in 1969. By then, I was in senior high, riding the raging storm of social revolution.

My dad drove Mother and us kids to the Daubert farm. Peter Daubert, or Tauber, came to America in 1742. He acquired the farm soon thereafter. Many German people came to Pennsylvania under Penn's 'experiment in religious freedom'.

When we arrived, the massive old stone house stood there as it always had. It was solid, enduring, wizened by centuries. Now its sturdy exterior belied what was to come. A heavy swell of loud, urgent German talk crashed over us like a breaking dam as we entered the kitchen door. Clearly there was serious trouble.

I retreated to a seat by the window, in a distant corner warmed by the old cook stove. I watched and listened for clues of the catastrophe that had apparently befallen Grandpa Joe's entire family.

The ever-present Deutsche cooking still perfumed the air. The gentle quality of dappled light down the hallway was just the same. Everything about the place looked to be in its usual order. Nothing I recalled had looked amiss outside the house.

Yet the boisterous joviality that had always flowed around the Daubert homestead had vanished. It appeared that no one was dead or dying. But the grief and tension that overtook the farmhouse sliced through my refusal to learn Grandpa's language. The anguish and anger, the worry and fear, engulfed me. It was like an alarming dream in which I had no voice. Grandpa's relatives were intent on discussion of the catastrophe. No one offered a translation.

The longer I waited for signs of what was wrong, the more the intensity of their voices frightened me. I longed for the old laughter and joking to begin, feasting on hardy farm 'eats'. Where was the usual Sunday loafing? But the laughter never came. I do not remember anyone eating a single bite of food. You must understand how rare that is in a Pennsylvania Deutsche farm kitchen.

Suddenly, we were leaving. On the winding drive home, I finally asked my father what was wrong. "If you learned Deutsche you would know," was his stiff response. I had been chastised and knew why. I lived among the Capps, and identified with my mother's people. That seemed to upset my father.

Now that I am grown and he is gone, I know my father was cut to the bone by the events that were to come. He could not avoid assessing these events as anything less than a betrayal of his father's ancestors.

Peter Daubert was wounded in the Revolutionary War, but he lived. I have seen the record of his disability pension. My father also saw the coming events as an insult to centuries of Daubert toil to feed the nation.

The jokes made by people in the bigger towns who thought themselves quite superior must have been stinging in his ears. These people ridiculed the Deutsche farm culture and made fun of the way its people spoke. They would say the farmers stank and called them stupid.

But my father loved his father's people. He was mourning a family history that could soon live only in photographs and memories.

The fact that I, his eldest child, had not taken interest in the Daubert's traditional language didn't help to soothe his sorrow a bit. How long he hid the terrible news, swaddled in the language of his father, I cannot recall. It is only the realization that he was gripped by grief that I remember.

The next time we went to the Daubert farm, it was not to see the relatives. They were not there. The ancient house of field stones was reduced to an astonishing heap of rubble. Government condemnation. Smashed beyond recognition by a wrecking ball.

The home that sheltered the Daubert kin since Peter and his brother left the Alsace-Lorraine in 1742 was gone forever. I was stunned. I stared in disbelief. It was like a corpse left to the whims of irreverent buzzards. Then I thought of the dismembered home in Indiantown my mother's people mourned. It would be many years before I learned it met an even more violent end.

Daddy said the Daubert's whole farming community would become a big recreation park for people from the city. The families who were not willing sellers were given no choice. The state condemned their farms and forced them out. Their houses were smashed with the wrecking ball or torched to the ground. Resistors would have no place to lay their heads.

Swatara Creek, the place of eels, was to be dammed for electricity. It would form a lake for those who could afford such amusements as boating and water skiing. The entire farm community would be covered over with recreational waters, never to be touched by the grandchildren.

This displacement of the unwilling, it insisted, was in the best interest of the whole people. So the farmers, the public was to believe, were simply being selfish in not wanting to sell their farms.

I wondered why the farmers and the food they grew were not more valued than convenience and leisure. And I wondered how even white people could be forced from their land. I asked, "Daddy, how can they do this?" "A wise man once said that absolute power corrupts absolutely," is what he said.

My father was an avid student of both Indian and American history. Both he and Mother were on their local Democrat committee, staunch advocates of civil rights. The rest of their relations tended toward the Republican party.

Some folks never forgot the infamous President Andrew Jackson's vicious Indian policy, and Jackson was a Democrat. Partisan matters had always led to some rather stimulating debate around our kitchen tables. But this power of condemnation was something new to me.

It was then that I struggled to absorb the biggest shock of my young life. I grew up knowing how hideously Indian people were treated. But this condemnation of Grandpa Daubert's family home was a total surprise. What was supposed to be government by and for the people, not only took land from Indian people, it continued to take from *whomever* it pleased. Even white people. This stunned me.

Not even people whose ancestors fought the American Revolution were immune. European colonization and anti-Indian sentiments, I realized, were apparently no longer the only factors that led to land grabs. There are powerful people who simply assume their plans for your land, no matter what your race, are so important that they will abuse their power in order to take it. I wandered away to be alone with the heaviness and confusion in my heart.

This new mystery of a power to seize any people's land was added to the mystery of Indiantown. I thought about the doctrine of manifest destiny. Here was a thing somehow similar, turned against non-Indian people and their land. My father called it the powers of eminent domain and government condemnation.

Knowing how this pained Grandpa's people, I thought back about the Indian removals and all the people that died in the fight for their lands. No farmers that I knew of had died like that in Suedberg in 1969. But what would have happened if the farmers refused to leave and fought back?

My parents' teaching about civil rights insisted on belief in justice for all. So, I knew this business of forcing unwilling farmers from their land was not just. Faced with this new reality, I felt like a child with only a stick to conquer the plague. Hot tears stung my eyes. The plague was even bigger than I'd thought.

- Chapter Two -

Westward Comes The Answer

The Mother's fertile soil and pungent humus cradle so many things, both those coming to the world and those passed on. Even a small child with a digging stick may discover and commit these things to memory. Early potatoes and fragrant roots. An ancient camp's discarded clamshells. Fantastic, eerie mushrooms resembling flesh and the ghostly looking Indian pipes that grow in the forest. Broken implements, shards of china, discarded bones and forgotten flint stones. These are the Earth child's playthings. They begin to convey the imagination from immediate curiosities to those concerning the greater dramas of humanity and life on this planet.

At the age of three with cowboy hat and six shooters, I galloped along on a big, white Wonder Horse named George. We made an incredible racket in the living room, tearing across the rugged black and white terrain of television Westerns. Roy Rogers and Dale Evans sang 'Happy Trails' to me every week like clockwork, but I soon knew George and I weren't really getting anywhere at all.

Daddy had given me a white Eskimo pup for my birthday. The intrepid Frosty became my real, live companion in constant jail-breaks from confinement in a safe little yard that had been fenced specifically to prevent our travels. Too many fascinating things beyond that fence beckoned for our attention. There were wild kittens to be captured in the haystacks, the blacksnake which lived in the corn crib, comedic pigs snorting at the trough and flapping, squawky chickens. We needed to visit Auntie picking dandelion, and the cousins down the road. Before long we were catching slippery salamanders and pinchy crayfish in the creek, riding horses, chasing errant milk cows, and exploring far from the sheltered little world of secret Indians in which I had been born.

18

The bike Dad had resurrected from the junkyard propelled me, along with cousin Judy, across country roads to old graveyards where we would read the headstones and wonder about the persons interred below. There were the houses rumored to be haunted, and sites claimed to be those of 'Indian massacres' of which my ancestors were accused. These are the sort of things that raise questions in the curious child's mind— questions about those that went before, how they lived and died, who they loved and who they may have even hated. What really propels the incessant migrations of hunters, gatherers and agrarian peoples rooted in the Earth? How in the world did our ancestors survive? Who are we, and why?

As a child who knew myself to be both Indian and white, nothing aggravated those questions more than Saturday morning TV. Week after week, year after year. Cowboys and Indians. Wagon trains and Indians. Cavalry and Indians. The fear, the hate and the fighting never seemed to stop. And the Indians never won on TV in those days. I wondered if there was a war in my bloodstream. Must there be winners and losers, or could we all somehow live in peace?

This Indian-ness versus white-ness was a topic of much discussion and speculation among myself and cousins Jim and Judy, my two most constant companions. We even knew some kids named Custer who claimed to be distant relations of the infamous George Armstrong Custer. That just made the whole dilemma seem all the more relevant to us.

From all I'd learned of human history as a young child, it seemed this fearing and hating and fighting - apparently always over territory - had gone on and on all over the whole planet for way too long. It wasn't just on TV and in the schoolbooks. In the Sunday schools, it certainly ran all through the Bible times.

Mother always had an inquiring mind. Among the treasures she possessed were fossils, a microscope, a meteorite and a telescope with which she searched the stars she knew so well for signs of distant life. This is a woman who, when she was pregnant with me, dissected a dead copperhead she'd found just for something

interesting to do. Mother was a language major who could still be
found most often behind a book. She read me Greek mythology
and Roman history in Latin, James Michenner adventures, stories
of Mexico in Spanish, and incredible tales of science fiction.

Everything in print, too, seemed to indicate this horrid business of
human strife over land had ancient roots and planned to keep right
on going into the future, to rocket right out into space itself. Sometimes the thought of this continual fighting and dehumanization of
one group of humans against the other was so disturbing that it
was hard to even think of having fun. I stewed over it so much
that Mother worried about me.

It always came back to the fact that we mortals kept making a
mess of things despite our best efforts. And, certainly, turning the
other cheek had often gotten people killed. Humanity appeared to
be a rather puny force that had somehow been sucked into a
voracious cycle of division and conquest. I figured maybe only
the Creator was powerful enough to ever fix this mess. And so it
was that I schemed to conduct a test asking tangible proof that
prayer works. It was my secret from the grown-ups; my plan
could get me scolded for questioning the Maker.

It wasn't a very sophisticated test, simply praying over and over
that night with all my muster, asking for the Creator give me a
white horse as a sign. Finally sleep overtook me, and next thing,
morning had come. A ripple of excitement, anticipation…and then
trepidation ran through me. What if it was wrong to ask such a
thing? Even worse, what if there was no answer?

Down the hall to breakfast I went, self-consciously burdened with
the weight of my own persistence. A bowl of cereal got casual
attention. Perhaps I'd risen late from staying awake so long the
night before. I sat there, thankfully alone, slipping eventually into
musing.

"Tiana!" Uncle Levi's voice jolted me back from my daydreams.
What? Someone calling me? Tiana is what the older folks called
me instead of Diana. "Tiana, come out here!" Uncle's voiced
plucked me from the table and out the back door.

There he stood, sparkling smile in his eyes, rope in hand…and at the end of that rope, a white mare. I flew off the porch, and had it not been for gravity, would probably have flown straight to the heavens, tragically consumed by the Great Mystery's inconceivable radiance. In short, no words could describe my awe.

"Tiana, I want to give you this horse," Uncle said. It seemed that bright light in his eyes was really the Creator speaking. Yes! The answer is yes! Then Mother emerged from the house asking what this was all about. "Uncle is giving me this horse!" tumbled from my mouth. Uncle verified it was so. He wished to give me Queenie, his white horse.

"You can't keep it," was her uncanny, flat-toned pronouncement. I could not believe my ears! Could Mother simply stand there wielding a raggedy old dishtowel, fix her hands on her hips, and cancel the Creator's action? Just like that? Nausea leaped into my stomach, rushing clear to my brain. A lump exploded in my throat that threatened to choke me to death right then and there. Mother says I cannot keep the white horse, the very answer to my prayer. How can this be?

Trying to conceal my panic, I asked, "Why can't I keep her?" Her explanation was equally unbelievable. "We can't afford the hay," mother said. What? Anger began to boil up in my heart. Her reason made no sense at all. She knew that the horse's hay was grown right there on the farm. How could she be so mean? I wanted to holler, but did not dare to lose any remaining chance of keeping the white horse.

Frantically casting around for some bulletproof reasoning to use with Mother soon led to recollection of what I had done to bring the situation on. Anger turned to sheepishness. My request was, to be given a white horse as proof that prayer works. There stood Uncle with the proof. Yet as quickly as I rejoiced in the proof, upon Mother's response I became filled with desire to *keep* it. I nearly forgot that I'd gotten my answer.

The white horse was in fact given. Yes, there is a line to the Creator's ear. Mother then gave the white horse back. Oh!…be humble with this power of speaking to the Maker. No further questions, Your Honor. I watched Uncle's back as he returned the horse to her pasture. I didn't *own* the white horse, but I had both my answer and a new name. Eventually the white horse returned in my dreams, and in time I would also find Uncle John's eagle. In the meantime, I really could see Queenie anytime along with all the other horses on the farm.

When I grew up, I purchased a house that was a genuine George-Washington-slept-here limestone inn on Old Route 422, just a few miles from the farm. There I kept a little antique shop. I'd taken a summer position at Hershey Museum of American Life. Giving tours and dusting artifacts led to yet more musing on the migrations and conflicts of man.

The American Indian section displayed an actual ancient Lenape burial inside a sealed glass case. It was a reminder of the disrespect the people received. The museum's insistence on displaying this deceased person who could have even been my ancestor sickened me so that I sometimes think the revulsion is what finally propelled me right out of the state. Within a year, firstborn child in tow, I moved to Washington, DC to pursue further education.

That city was an education in itself, from Smithsonian Institution and massive halls of the federal government, to the international community and homeless street people playing traffic director on 14th and Pennsylvania Avenue. I met the Immigration and Naturalization Service chief who came to the school to speak on US policy regarding the throngs of humanity still hungry to migrate to America, and had to work with the US Department of Health, Education and Welfare. It was there that I marched in the streets for human rights.

My work as assistant director of student financial aid at an alternative liberal arts college, staffed mostly by old Peace Corps people, was with a majority of international and black inner city students. There I met black Indians for the first time. I received my first death threat from a white political radical—a fellow who insisted on a student loan even though he said he would never pay it back. Most amazing was my totally entertaining secretary, Yvon, a drama student. Growing up in DC, she divulged, she didn't know until near adulthood that milk comes from cows. Wow, culture shock. We had some uproarious times.

A promotion to department director soon distracted from my own education. I looked west to Olympia, Washington, on Puget Sound, to the Evergreen State College. Evergreen was also called 'the environmental hippie school'. Evergreen students were called 'Greeners'.

The Endangered Species Act was in its infancy. Indian religion was legalized in 1978, four years after the Pacific Northwest was rocked by the Boldt Decision. Apex of the Northwest salmon wars, the Boldt Decision gave certain federally recognized treaty tribes fifty percent of the salmon harvest. It was a decision even the Indians didn't expect.

At Evergreen there were few international students or students of color, but a lot more homegrown hippie radicals than in DC. I was a visual arts major-psychology minor who apparently possessed a talent to embarrass even the notoriously liberal Evergreen administration with frankly visceral art exhibitions. Back then, I got into constructing environments relating to human cultures, human rights and women's themes. I turned-out pieces like the filthy, percolating "Detoxification Chamber" and writhing, life size ceramic snakes featured in rape theme scenarios, the 40 foot womb simulation called "Lub Dub Mama" and ridiculous mock surgery gizmos dangling from the bedspring ceiling of "I'll Have a June Bride and a Pink Lady, Please".

It wasn't pretty art. But if controversy is any measure of success, it was darned successful. Somehow I always managed to take logic and instinct so far down the radical road that it flew clear off the group think radar. No cozy niche, no follower, nobody's fool. I grew up in a household where lively debate, especially political and philosophical debate, was elevated to a family sport, with breaks for additional research to prove our points. I really appreciate my parents for encouraging me to challenge even my own thinking. That nose for hypocrisy saved my hide from membership in many a political club.

Ensconced amid several hundred acres of cedar giants, life at environmental central was really very insulated from everyday people. Remember the old song that went "I love everyday people..."? Well, Greener environmentalists typically believed they were saving the planet for everyday people—those they saw as the intellectually disadvantaged masses they would rescue from massive corporations and capitalism itself.

Respecting Mother Earth, and protecting the environment for the sake of the whole human family is a very worthy goal. However, there were a few disturbing things going on in the name of Mother Earth. For one, the eco-warriors' lumped the *everyday* family farmer right in there with the corporate fat cats. Eastern tribal peoples were farmers. My family used nothing but manure and lime on our fields, kept large portions of the farm in woodlands, and plowed nowhere near the creeks. The Pennsylvania Deutsche, too, were wonderful caretakers of the land. This is how the farms I grew up around operated.

The book, *Where's The Food?*, made it very clear that huge agri-chemical companies and their banking partners were wiping out family farms left and right. People claiming concern about pro-moting more natural food production and crop variety should have been supporting family farms and ranches, not demonizing them. Respecting Mother Earth was right down my alley, but I wasn't into blindly marching behind city-born gurus who characterized farmers as rapists of the planet.

Another very disturbing thing was the environmentalists' appro-priation and re-interpretation of all things Indian. Remember the old TV commercial, the one that depicted old Iron Eyes Cody crying about pollution? It was pretty insulting to some people. Some felt it emasculated Indian men. Others felt the ad's use of Indians as mascots was degrading and disempowering. Yet this kind of thing continued.

What about Indigenous American peoples' need to eat meat and fish? In addition to hunting and fishing rights being important as-pects of culture and self-determination, the consumption of meat and fish is absolutely essential to their health. Yet so many ecological activists were and still are totally opposed to this. That kind of thinking is just plain genocidal.

It is even more disturbing now to look back on the way these privileged environmentalists courted Indian peoples' favor. In a twisted way, they try to use their environmental war to pardon their own sense of guilt, excuse their own denied racism, and convince even themselves they are just as oppressed as Indians have been. It may be more charitable to say they are trying to be friends, but it looks like that same old friendship that's based on using people less fortunate to get ahead.

Maybe it was bound to happen in the social climate after the 60's. So many young white people rejected their hereditary culture and religion. Young Indian people were by then found in greater numbers in cities and universities, questioning the dominant society, and seeking long delayed justice. The new age environmentalist appeals I heard went something like this—

'Hey, man, like, you can trust us, we're the good white people. We disagree with everything our ancestors have ever done. In fact we're not really white at all, we're Indians reborn in white bodies. Really. It says so in this book I read. It's like this really groovy cosmic plan, man, so that we could come back and help you. We're just here with our attorneys and our superior knowledge of the system to, like, save you and save Mother Earth, too. Just let us put your sacred symbols on our literature and your sad little red faces on our posters. Together we can win this, man. Red Power. Right on. You know, man, like, be our sacred environmental mascots. We love you and the Earth Mother. We're victims of the white man just like you. Just fight for the planet with us and like, let us use your treaty rights in our lawsuits to get rid of your white neighbors, man, those bad fishermen and miners and farmers and ranchers and loggers. Just march behind our Earth Day flag and we'll help you make the Ghost Dance come true.'

'Oh, and like you really gotta take us into your sweat lodge, man, and show us how to use your sacred pipe. Cause, like

*we really need your powerful medicine to win the war for the
Mother Earth, you know? We really wouldn't need you to do
this for us, man, except we had to come back in these white
bodies so we could help you save the planet. And it's because
of that, bro, that we had to have these really rich capitalist
pig parents, you know, so we could get educated and help
you. It's all really cosmic, man. Give us your medicine, show
us how it works, and we'll like, restore Turtle Island to pre-
European conditions. We'll give it all back to you, man. I
swear we will.*

*Of course we'll stay on the land with you. After all, we are
really white Indians and we saved the Earth Mother and did
all these wonderful things just for you. (Besides, you will still
need our scientific expertise to tell you how to do things right.)
Just sign here. We'll even get you some grant money, man.
Just sign here and then go line up with all the other folks who
love the planet. You can even bring your Indian flag with
you. That'll look good. Cool. Wow. All right, you won't
regret this. Really.'*

That's the basic pitch in a nutshell. You can easily imagine what a
rocky 'friendship' it has been. There is a good bit of controversy
in Indian country over non-Indian and even indigenous people like
the late well-known Vincent "Sun Bear" LaDuke. Outrage is
expressed at those who others believe profit wrongly by catering
to these very kinds of people. I knew LaDuke myself, and had
said I was not comfortable with the idea of being what I call an "8
x 10 Glossy Medicine Show".

I was taught that spirit gives its gifts, so healing and spiritual things
are not sold, but given where appropriate. Indian religion should
never be for sale, and I would think that people of other religions
would find this offensive, too. The subject of appropriation of
indigenous intellectual and cultural property is a subject taken seriously these days. Indian country is grappling both with surviving
modern economic realities and insuring respect for their cultures.

Look back in environmental literature over time—there's a lot of
posturing about what has been done to the Indian people. This is

especially so in the early deep ecology literature. Deep ecology eventually showed an anti-Indian, anti-human face. Yet it made sure to equate its environmental warnings with the holocaust of the Indian nations. One could easily conclude they were even trying to make Indians themselves feel guilty of raping Mother Earth if they wanted to use the earth's resources.

It was very important to them that they presented themselves as the ones who would save both the earth *and* the Indian. Indian treaty rights and legal status as harmed parties could help win environmental lawsuits. Yet there never has been near as much reward for the Indian as there is for the non-Indian environmentalists in this arrangement.

My question is, exactly what is the environmental majority envisioning for Indian land when they're done saving all the 'non-Indian land'? Can you trust people who all think they - not you - know the best way to use your land? The rhetoric in support of tribal self-determination loses its shine when Indians don't conform to environmental dogma.

If the Sierra Club's attitude toward the White Earth Land Recovery Project is any indication, it's not a very good sign. According to indigenous environmental justice activist Winona LaDuke, the Sierra Club opposed her tribe taking over management of a portion of former tribal land they're trying to buy back from the government. On top of that, The Nature Conservancy purchased 400 acres of land on her reservation and gave it to the state of Minnesota rather than the tribe.

Recently, Sierra Club announced its opposition to a land exchange between the Eastern Band of Cherokee in North Carolina and the National Park Service. The tribe needs the land to build schools where the tribe intends for children to learn about the natural environment. This opposition, even more curiously, defies the fact that NPS is actually set to get the better end of the bargain.

Those who eventually became the environmental leadership now collect huge six figure salaries while the same old poverty continues for so many Indian people. Unemployment throughout the remote rural reservations is especially overwhelming. I attended a memorial for Anna Mae Aquash on the Pine Ridge Reservation many years ago that began to familiarize me with very real problems like uranium, nuclear, and chemical contamination on the Western reservations. These problems *still* remain. A little bone is tossed to activists seeking justice for this mess, but the privileged environmental mainstream don't bother to mount the major coalitions they are quite capable of in order to help.

At the Environmental Grantmakers Association fall retreat in 1992, LaDuke pointed out this disparity quite clearly when she reminded the attendees that indigenous environmental groups received only 2/10 of 1% of the funding provided by EGA foundations for environmental organizations. By 1996, referring to the potential for alliances with the environmental mainstream, LaDuke stated, "While there is great potential for these strategies, there has been a very awkward courtship between Native environmental groups and larger environmental organizations." (*The Growing Strength of Native Environmentalism*, W. LaDuke)

Awkward courtship, indeed. Nothing has really changed over the years. While considering potential alliance, one could also conclude there is more potential for native groups to be used by environmental elitists. The mainstream groups continue to focus on what is to their political and financial advantage, and toss a little bone to indigenous groups once in a while.

There is an illusion of concern. Even the most serious toxics issues get little mainstream attention. It's hard *not* to conclude that their only interest is keeping indigenous groups waiting in the wings so that a few Indians can be trotted out when the environmental mainstream finds it convenient.

The environmental mainstream, I think, is rather haughty to portray itself as more powerful than Mother Earth by claiming to be saving *her*. They started out, actually, trying to save themselves. It all began with concerns about which manmade chemical substances did and did not pose a toxic danger to *humanity*. It's turned into a bunch of rich folks paid by even richer folks to claim they have to save Mother Earth by getting rid of people. It might have remained more honest if it had not become a big money industry. But nobody saw that coming back in the 70's. Most people still don't know.

Here's another perspective: Mother Earth is powerful. She will remain and spawn new life even if we destroy ourselves. Not a pretty picture, but many old religious traditions say it has happened before. It is ourselves, humanity, that we must save from the same old elitist, plutocratic land grabbing mentality that has oppressed the masses, disrespected human rights and despoiled nature with impunity throughout the history of civilization. So the big question is—*who* will determine *how* to do this? The privileged class? I hope not— that's who got us where we are.

Well, alas, the day arrived for me to leave Evergreen's intellectual cocoon. My sculpture professor that year flatly opined that school was not the place for me anymore. He said it was time for me to get out in the world and take it on. He was right. I was out of money.

Seattle. Bookstores perfumed with espresso. Brass railed waterfront bars. High dollar art galleries, Chinatown and missions snagging lost Indians were all encased in the same damp fog of fish scented air. On the streets of Seattle, on the docks and the beaches, I wondered if my feet touched a place Uncle John had stood. He took his final road trip in '74, the journey to the spirit world.

Some things that change your life come right out of nowhere. That's how the conversation with Grandma Lillian came about. I had a dream about my grandma dying. After waking from the dream, I phoned Mother. "Is Grandma OK?" On the other end so far away, "Well she has her diabetes, but she's fine." I called Grandma anyway, just to hear her voice.

The conversation came around - same old me - to the same old question. "Grandma, why did we leave Indiantown Gap?" But now, Grandma was finally talking. "The government wanted our land. They said everybody had to sell their land," she said.

"But, Grandma, did we *want* to sell our land?" (I knew that couldn't be so.) "No, *we* didn't want to sell our land," she said, "but some of the people did sell their land. They said they knew what would happen if they didn't, so they sold their land. But we didn't want to leave there. It was *our* land, so we stayed. But some people sold their land."

"So why *did* we leave the Valley, Grandma?"

"Well, we didn't want to leave the Valley. But if we didn't leave, they would have killed us all. They sent the National Guard in after us. We didn't know they were coming. They came into the Valley real fast in their big army trucks full of soldiers. They didn't care *who* they hurt. They were chasing people down the road with their big trucks. We couldn't get away from them, they would have killed us all."

Grandma started to say what happened to one man, but her voice cracked. It is the only time in my whole life I ever heard her cry. "We had to leave, Tiana. We loved the Valley. We didn't want to go."

I asked why no one would tell me why we left when I was a kid. "We were afraid," she said. "We knew how you were. We were afraid you would talk. We were afraid of what they would do to you. We were afraid of what they would do to all of us."

It is true that in childhood my seemingly uncontrollable urges to speak the truth created awkward moments. But the reason we left Indiantown had been kept from all the children, beginning with my mother who was only two years old when it happened. So, Grandma must have decided the time had finally come to end the silence. Truth has a life of its own—Grandma released it from captivity.

In those few moments I understood so much more about my mother's people than ever before. Most of all, why they remained secret Indians all those years. It had already become a well-worn pattern of Indian survival in the East, concealing themselves in the forests and mountains, and finally, amidst the dominant society itself. This is how we resisted numerous campaigns of removal. Secrecy had come to mean life itself.

We never wanted to leave the Valley. We were not willing sellers of our land. We had no choice. None. At least our more immediate family was still together.

Yet one would have to leave us. That is how Uncle John became the traveling man. He was 32 years old when Indiantown Gap was lost to us in 1932. When World War II came along, John was drafted, but he soon hit the rails. The taking of our land was still too bitter a pill for him to swallow.

At first Uncle would come home to the farm every time he went AWOL. But it scared the children each time the MP's came around with their guns drawn. They were rough and threatening when they came to search the house and farm for the renegade John Capp. For the sake of the children, Uncle John left his family and homeland. He took to hopping freight trains. He lived his whole life traveling back and forth from his homeland to Puget Sound, and the four quarters of Turtle Island.

There *was* one Capp, Grandma told me, who evaded the removal from Indiantown Gap, held her ground and was never driven out of the Blue Mountains. My Great Great Aunt Anne escaped the removal. Her little old time cabin was hidden way up on the mountain—just Auntie, her chickens, and her pet rattlesnakes living under the porch. Aunt Anne lived the old way. She had no need to leave the mountain. Some people were afraid of old auntie's traditional ways, Grandma told me, but the family loved her dearly. Grandma said the family visited her secretly whenever they could after they were forced out of the Valley.

The year after the soldiers chased us out, Grandma had told me, they used our house for artillery practice. Perhaps Aunt Anne herself was watching. Maybe that is how the relatives knew. That, and the day the soldiers came, must have been in their thoughts every day. It is no wonder the air was so thick with unanswered questions each time they visited the Valley to remember the old life.

This is what a state website says about the acquisition of Indiantown Gap—

"Development of the military reservation at Indiantown Gap was completed by the Commonwealth of Pennsylvania from 1930-1941, and today it serves as headquarters for the Pennsylvania National Guard and a regional hub for Guard, reserve and active component training. A great deal of history lies in the 19,000-acre post in Lebanon County now called Fort Indiantown Gap.

The name Indiantown was derived from the four Indian villages in the vicinity and the name Indiantown Gap is derived from a separation in the Blue Mountains, one of several used by Indians as a throughway to Shamokin. Pioneers of Scotch-Irish, English and German descent settled in this region around 1738 and worked hard to clear the fields and eke out a living, co-existing with the friendly Lenape Indians.

A section of Route 22 that goes by Fort Indiantown Gap was once an Indian trail. When the settlers came to this vicinity, it became a wagon road, then it was taken over by the stagecoaches, and eventually a highway was constructed over top of the old patch. But just as the settlers were gaining a foothold, the French and Indian War broke out, and roving bands of Indians plagued the settlers, scalping men, women and children, setting fire to their log homes and barns. The Indiantown Gap area was considered the high-water mark of the French and Indian War, and many forts and blockhouses were built in the vicinity, including the Swatara Fort, Harpers Fort and Reeds Fort.

When the Pennsylvania National Guard needed a larger area for their training maneuvers and firing ranges than the military reservation it was using at Mount Gretna, authorization was made to acquire 12,047 acres of land in Dauphin and Lebanon Counties. The entire package of land was acquired in 1931 for $308,944, and many of the farmhouses and outbuildings from those acquisitions are still in use around the installation. Fort Indiantown Gap was used for the first time

*by the 55ᵗʰ Infantry Brigade for its annual maneuvers at the
reservation in the summer of 1932. The following year the
53ʳᵈ Field Artillery took its training here, and in 1934 the 28ᵗʰ
Infantry Division and 52ⁿᵈ Cavalry Brigade were assembled
at the Gap. Over 100 buildings— including officers' mess
halls, office buildings, latrines and bath houses — were dis-
mantled and hauled on flatbed trucks from the limited quarters at Mount Gretna to the present location at Fort Indiantown
Gap. Additional land was purchased later."*

Read carefully: "A great deal of history lies in the 19,000-acre
post... authorization was made to acquire 12,047 acres of
land...The entire package of land was acquired in 1931 for
$308,944... Fort Indiantown Gap was used for the first time by
the 55ᵗʰ Infantry Brigade for its annual maneuvers at the reservation in the summer of 1932... The following year the 53ʳᵈ Field
Artillery took its training here... Additional land was purchased
later."

Apparently my mother's people served as live subjects for the
55ᵗʰ Infantry Brigade's field maneuvers in the summer of 1932.
That is the year Grandma said the soldiers suddenly descended
and forced them out. I do not know yet where the soldiers took
them that day. We moved into the new farm in October of 1932.
Our homes and barns served as real targets for the 53ʳᵈ Field
Artillery in 1933.

We were not willing sellers of our land, our communities, our security, our culture, or our history. Who will replace all the things
we lost on that terrifying day in 1932? Who will heal the terror of
that day and every day thereafter?

The older people in Grandpa Daubert's family may have known
about this when the government came along thirty seven years
later wanting *their* farmland. Suedberg is not far at all from
Indiantown Gap. They may also have been remembering a time
during World War II when speaking the local's old traditional dia-
lect of Pennsylvania German was judged dangerously anti-Ameri-
can. That must have been both humiliating and terrifying to the
Pennsylvania's old German speaking farm communities. No won-

der the news of condemnation had fallen so alarmingly upon their ears, and landed so heavily in their hearts.

It seemed the same old mindset of manifest destiny had simply continued to consume land, and the people of that land, in the name of 'public good' and eminent domain. The power of land condemnation is indeed as awful as it sounds.

Little did I realize even then that - in addition to all the Indian land that was taken through war, allotment and termination - the National Parks and many public works of the New Deal era were also established by taking land from unwilling rural people. Back then many mountain people of the east - Indian and non-Indian - were forced from their land in the name of conservation, tourism and the public good.

The history books gloss over a long trail that began in America circa 1492. From the original shameless conquest of the Indian nations on, a pattern of violating the human rights of indigenous and other rural peoples has developed. The elite class simply turns public opinion against whatever people's land they want. They invariably claim they are merely looking after the greater public good.

However, the financial benefits to the elite class are immense, while the unwilling sellers are given no choice and an unfair price. The unwilling are demonized, accused of endangering the public's welfare. Thus they are driven from the land—despised, cheated and dispossessed.

It is part of a larger pattern that encompasses the war against the Indian nations. There is a pattern of political-economic domination over the inhabitants of the rural landscape throughout the history of human civilization. In that sense it is a very ancient war that has clearly never really ended.

In America today the public clings to the myth that the Indian wars are over, as well as the myth that all government land acquisitions are purchased from willing sellers and are for the greater public's good. They cling to these myths until the day they themselves receive some shocking notice from government agents proving them wrong.

Perhaps they are told their home interferes with the scenic "viewshed", that it somehow harms the greater public's enjoyment of a natural or historical area, or that their land is to become a repository for society's most dangerous waste. There are so many reasons today, as there have always been, for removing, relocating and parting land-based people from the land. Yet it is the same old war that never ended wherein the political-economic elite have their way with the rural peoples that have throughout time clung to the land.

-Chapter Three-

All This Way On A Quarter

Sometimes a human being must retreat deep into the forest. The truth about Indiantown Gap penetrated my whole world. The awful pain in Grandma's voice filled my head. It was time to let go of everything but my children, to find my way forward.

We camped in the off-season, in the heart of the vast Olympic Peninsula, staying longest in the cool shadows of the Dungeness River. The children attended the school of nature. Our 55 gallon stock tank over the campfire served as a tub to scrub my wild little offspring clean. We had the river for music and each other for company. The ravens teased just like my aunties and uncles. On a quiet night, one of the stick Indians so many believe are myth danced mischievously through camp. One is never really alone.

After a few months, a work opportunity arose from a temporary Indian Health Service contract with a dentist friend. We were to cover Nisqually and Skokomish dental clinics on the southern end of Puget Sound. We camped on the Nisqually rez and the river for a few months, then moved with the fall rains to a cozy little house on a remote, forested shore. Between the Skokomish and Squaxin Island reservations, there was more solitude and all the meaty chantrelle mushrooms one cares to eat.

One fine day, through the unremarkable trailer door of the Skokomish dental clinic, walked a remarkable new friend. Come the season, Carol Lee invited me to the winter dance ceremonial in her Skokomish people's Big House. I thank her, again.

Words can not describe how it felt to first sit on the plank benches of the old time Big House, drenched in the booming voices of song

and thunderous drums forbidden back home for so many years.
Only those who have experienced it can imagine the deep wounds
inflicted on a people who are denied by force their religious and
cultural traditions. In the heavy woodsmoke atmosphere of that
Skokomish Big House, I had just begun to understand Uncle John's
words.

After the IHS contract, I joined friends up north on Fidalgo Island.
Through Joe Waterhouse, a Klallum, and a former Greener like
myself, I met Ken Hansen, chairman of the Samish Tribe, and his
Coast Salish relatives there and on Vancouver Island. Through
Ken and his relatives I continued to attend the winter ceremonials.
These were good traditional people, and that was very fortunate
for me. The Coast Salish are related to the Lenape from ancient
times when the Lenape first migrated across the continent thousands of years ago.

The windswept islands of Puget Sound seemed to spit out ancient
stone implements right and left, like the fields back home. On the
beaches I thought about the migrations and movements of peoples
across the Earth and time. Here I stood upon the same land my
ancient ancestors also stood upon, as they also had in Pennsylvania where I was born. What unforeseen migrations might be yet
to come? I thought about Uncle John standing on these shores.

Holed up one afternoon in the Samish tribal center with a big,
hefty art book, I studied page after page of ancient eastern woodland Indian objects. War clubs, sacred pipes, ancient pots, retired
moccasins. Contorted Cayuga false face masks. The Lenape big
house interior with its carved posts. Turning the next page, I gasped
involuntarily at the sight of a red and black Lenape split face mask,
the face of Mesingw (Misinkhâlikàn), with deer hide hair. He
was the ancient giver of the Lenape Big House ceremony.

I felt profoundly lonely, physically homesick like it was coming out
of my bones. As time passed, the Indian doctors concluded that I
was not physically ill, but Indian sick. Like labor that is suddenly
upon a birthing mother, the process of inheriting what the Coast
Salish with whom I then lived called seowin songs, the Big House
songs of my own ancestors, had begun. I will always be thankful

for the good help of Issadore Thom, Tommy Paul, Clyde and
Marilyn Jack, Ken Hansen, their families and relatives, at that
time. They were so kind to this strange 'orphan' relative from a
distant time and place.

That quarter Great Uncle John gave me as a little girl had resulted
in a pretty long ride— all the way to Puget Sound, to the secret of
Indiantown, the old time Big House and the songs of our ancestors. It was just as he said. Now it seemed that a circle was
closing. In the spring I loaded up the kids for a road trip to the
homeland, the rolling Appalachian hills and mountains that still held
my heart and the bones of my ancestors in the East.

We took the southern instead of the northern route this time, passing through California and the Southwest, then through Oklahoma
where many of the eastern tribal people ended up. We stopped in
Alabama for a long visit with a friend whose mother was a wonderful old Cherokee woman from Tennessee. The red earth is so
beautiful there in Alabama.

Still incredibly energetic in her seventies, Mary Lou had, single-
handed, remodeled her homey old farmhouse. She is possibly the
only person to ever seriously describe a baby cottonmouth as 'soooo
cute'. She even let a copperhead live under her porch. I was
reminded of Aunt Anne. It made me wonder if she was alone
with her rattlesnakes on the mountain at the Gap when she finally
passed on.

Visiting our Valley, back in Pennsylvania, I mourned what happened there and the obvious improbability of ever regaining that
land. Getting land back from the military was simply unheard of.
Yet the Gap always seemed plagued with financial shortfalls and
rumors that it might close shop. It was so disheartening. So were
the tracts of upscale suburban housing set on generous lots that
came to insinuate themselves all over the farm on which I had
grown up.

Many of the surrounding farms had also been squeezed out. Just
how many of the farms in Lebanon, Dauphin, and perhaps other
counties were inhabited by other refugee families from Indiantown

Gap, I still did not know. It surely seemed as though someone else's vision for the land, quite alien to my own kin, pursued us wherever we went. I felt like I was adrift.

Surprisingly, it was also still possible to visit the heap of stoney rubble that was once Grandpa Daubert's family farmstead. Oddly enough, though fifteen years had passed, the state still had not dammed the Swatara or flooded all those old farms they had condemned against the wishes of their unwilling sellers.

Environmentalists had delayed the dam since 1969 because they wanted to study the gypsy moth. Yet they didn't care to allow the farmers back on their farms. Instead the fields were growing over and the area bore no marker to even speak of what had happened there. It was as though Grandpa's community had also 'never existed'. Now Swatara State Park was one more vast tract of government owned land seized from people with no choice.

Visiting the homeland was a mixed bag of joy and grief. Some of the relatives wanted to hear what Uncle John's instructions had produced. Some were not so enthusiastic. I saw no sign as yet that the Lenape people of Pennsylvania had come out of their long hiding. More than ever, I felt like a misplaced anthropological artifact, like the lonely bones in the Hershey Museum...like a ghost.

On the return trip to Washington state, again in Alabama, I dreamed of rushing home to meet my elders. It certainly made me wonder why I was, in waking reality, once again headed three thousand miles in the opposite direction.

-Chapter Four-

Same Old Land Grabbing Hand

Right along the Canadian border, in the vast openness of North-east Washington, Ferry County is a rather remote mountain place most folks have never even heard of, much less seen. The families here in this isolated country still gather firewood to heat their homes, hunt to augment the food budget, and pick huckleberries and mushrooms in the wild terrain which surrounds them. They have always made their living at the traditional rural occupations - ranching, timber and mining - like any remotely located Western community.

The families in Ferry County are quite literally dependent upon the land for their survival. They're not the big industry fat cats that urban people are told about, they're generational rural folks just trying to raise their families. Just like all rural cultures throughout history, without access to the land, these communities simply could not exist.

The county consists of 1.4 million acres and a sparse 7,200 people in the Kettle Mountains. But only 15% of the land is private property, so 85% is government controlled. The south half of the county is the eastern half of the reservation for the Colville Confederated Tribes, under the federal Bureau of Land Management, and almost all the north half is part of the Colville National Forest, managed by the US Forest Service.

Tribal land, of course, is supposed to be managed for the good of the tribe, and many years ago when the National Forests were established, the US Forest Service was also charged with providing for the stability of the rural communities that live among and work on these lands. The National Forests were initially supposed to have been established to make sure the people of the US always have a secure and sustainable supply of wood.

Timber and livestock grazing have provided for several generations of rural people on both halves of Ferry County. In fact, Lucy Covington of the Colvilles financed her vital trips to Washington, DC, to win the fight against termination of their reservation, with the sale of her cattle. Most urban folks don't realize that a lot of Indians in the West ranch and log for a living, too. Colville Reservation ranch families are represented by the Colville Indian Livestock Association, just like ranchers throughout the west are represented by local livestock or cattlemen's associations.

It was interesting for me to learn that those who study indigenous languages say the interior Salish language in this area is related to the Lenape language back east, from some time far, far in the distant past. It is not so hard to understand the Indian expression 'we are all related' when we look on things like this.

Now we live in a world where people of all the racial groups are living on every continent. This, combined with rapid and expansive changes in technology, may indicate that we are living in a substantially remarkable moment in the history of human civilization. Significant change for all of humanity is bound to come from such a development.

Will this change ultimately be positive or negative for Earth and her peoples? This is no time for empty old rhetoric, dogma and rigid thinking where human rights activism is concerned. It is a time to be alert to the patterns forming that we might miss if we cling too tightly to our established assumptions. Many people warn about 'earth changes' that will come about as a spiritual and physical consequence of man's abuse of the earth. Some also believe we could prevent this by changing our ways.

Sadly, most people are not even aware of the worst abuses of our environment that have already taken place through secretive military-industrial experimentation and testing. We only have the opportunity to learn about such things when they are old news, and the deed is done. All the while, new secret projects are hidden from public knowledge. This makes the task of changing our ways on the planet especially difficult.

Humanity's abuse of humanity is another thing they say will bring about these earth changes. This problem, I believe, is at the heart of the whole matter. When corrupt plutocrats abuse land-based peoples, the land is also abused because the people of the land and the land itself are interconnected. Disrespect for the earth and disrespect for her children become one and the same. You can think about these things a lot when you live in solitude, far up on a mountain.

Lone Ranch Creek has a kind of ring to it that matches its quiet beauty. That's where my kids and I were by 1995. We lived in a rustic - no modern conveniences - octagonal log cabin adjacent to the Colville National Forest on the north half of Ferry County. Almost like a Hobbit house, this magical little place in the woods belonged to a local gal descended from Chiefs Long Alec and Tonasket. Even though she was living out of state, she hung on to this connection to her family, and I was the current guardian.

Just the year before, Mother sent a newspaper clipping from the Lebanon Daily News in Pennsylvania. The headlines read something like 'Indian Drums Heard Again at Indiantown Gap'. My eyes and heart just about popped out. The article said there had been a powwow held at Indiantown Gap Military Reservation. But there was no mention of the people who had lived at the Gap back in 1932.

However, there was news about the Indian people in Pennsylvania beginning to emerge. The news lingered in the back of my mind after so many years of what sometimes seemed like my exile in the West. Neither the memory of the fantastic colors of Appalachian autumns, the scent of the creeks, the gorgeous caverns, nor that inexplicable yearning one has for the land of one's childhood, had faded over the years of my absence.

For the time being, however, different from my homeland as it is, Eastern Washington would have to remain my surrogate mother. It's like dry, mountain desert country, really. It varies from piney scented forest to grasslands to pungent smelling sagebrush, with the heady perfume of cedars in the wet creek valleys, and lush grasses with cottonwood and willows on the creeks in the lowlands. It is cold as one would ever want to get in the winter, with mummifying heat in the summer. Life at the cabin on Lone Ranch Creek was rugged but quiet, except for the yearly invasion of urban hunters. That solitude suited me just fine.

Down by the creek one day, I heard a vehicle pull off the dirt road that ran through our place and on up through the National Forest. A young blonde, bearded fellow soon came down the bank to the creek. He said he was from Fish and Wildlife, and asked if he could take water samples from the creek. I told him that I only rented the place, but couldn't see the harm. I told him about how healthy the creek was, pointing out the fish and going on about how the cows help so much to prevent wildfire and hold back noxious weed invasion with their grazing. He got a quizzical look on his face, then went about his business of collecting water. I never thought another thing of it, not even when I saw him return to the creek on several more occasions in the coming weeks.

I'll never forget the day I met Curly Grumbach. He's one of the local ranchers who graze their cattle on the National Forest range up above the cabin where I lived. Some of his cows had gotten through the old fence around our horse pasture, which could hardly be helped with the rickety condition our fence was in. It was only politeness and hay, really, that kept my horses in there. As I drove down Lone Ranch Creek Road headed for town in my ancient Jeep, I noticed that Curly was rounding up cows. So I stopped to tell him he could find some of his cows in my pasture.

I guess he thought at first that I just wanted to complain about cows like so many outsiders who move into the rural West do. The first words out of his mouth were, "You people from California..." Well, Curly let me know just exactly what he thinks of the encroachments and attitudes of urban people from places like California who really don't know a thing about rural matters.

I told Curly that I was just a farm kid who'd been squeezed out of my homeland in Pennsylvania and had utter sympathy for his predicament. Watching your way of life be attacked and exterminated by haughty folks who understand much less than they imagine is a horrible fate to endure. I told him it seems to me that farmers need to prove with their own unbiased science that they are better environmentalists than the environmentalists are.

That they are better environmentalists I never had any doubt, based on the farming life in which I grew up. Farm people know every little inch of their land and all the creatures within it. They're out there in it all the time. It is their home. They take just as much pride in the health of the land and the wildlife as they do in the health of their herds and crops. And any real country person can tell you that wildlife loves farmers, because farmers grow really yummy food that wildlife thrives on.

PETA and the Animal Liberation Front may hate ranchers, but bald eagles love them. Eagles don't give a rip about political correctness, or even being icons, for that matter. But they do love to eat. There's nothing they enjoy better than a lazy meal of bovine afterbirth in the early spring calving season. They hang around the calving grounds and wait for the blessed event. Really!

I challenge you to find the mule deer that doesn't prefer the rancher's prize winning alfalfa field to strictly wild fare. That's why urban hunters get so spitting mad when they realize that they're really not allowed to hunt on private property without permission. Bambi's in Joe Rancher's alfalfa field!

Only a sorely misinformed urbanite or heartless land thief could fail to see how deeply farm families love the land and strive to preserve it for future generations. To do otherwise is against the nature of a farmer - not the caricature corporate fat cat - but a real live tractor driving farmer with a family and grandchildren he hopes will also farm the land his grandfathers farmed.

That's just what country people do. They respect the circle of life, and love the natural world they live in.

In 1997 it was a sad occasion that took me home to Pennsylvania for the brief week with my father that my finances could afford. Diagnosed too late with cancer, my dad would pass on within a year. It was almost beyond comprehension to see the strength drained from such a creative, energetic man, to see him confined in frustrating premature old age and frailty. He had always been a man of many projects, and now he could do none of them.

Yet Dad exuded quiet happiness when he showed me the circle of stone he had placed in the back yard. He had found these rocks through his dreams, he said, before his illness took hold. He told me that after all these years he had finally found his Lenape identity, a thing one would not normally even question if they'd seen him, his mother and siblings. Maybe the Moravians had converted his mother's people at an early date. They didn't live in the mountains like my mother's people. They lived the 'civilized life' in Reading, and then Lebanon.

So my father learned late in life what his family had hidden from him. Somehow this made him feel whole even though he was dying. This is what the fear and secrecy back east that prevailed, for so many years, did to countless Indian people. First the secrecy was just for survival. But soon, many people do not even know who they are, a mystery to even themselves. This loss of identity causes the people themselves to get lost. It is not a light matter.

Here near the end of his life, my father seemed to be at peace. As the plane that would take me back to my own children pulled away from Harrisburg International Airport, I watched him every last moment possible— standing there behind the big glass windows, smiling, waving, and fading from my life as he was also fading from the physical world. The day he died he passed by to check on me as he traveled to the spirit world, yet another ancestor whose dreams are passed to the next generation. He always told me to follow my dreams.

Late in the fall of 1998, a poster appeared in tiny little Curlew that caused quite a buzz. It was a big map that showed all the roads up in the National Forest above Lone Ranch that it said the Forest Service was planning to close. To people who rely on the woods for their firewood and their living, people who go to the woods to play and to rest their weary souls, being shut out of the woods is a terrible development.

This road closure business didn't sound good. You need to understand, these are skinny little dirt roads in the hills that only locals use, not the hardtop speedways a city slicker would imagine. I was living on a different mountain by then, but decided I'd better attend this meeting in town where the local Forest Service officials would speak, and see what this was all about.

That meeting was the event that opened my eyes about what had become of environmentalism. Before that, I thought the environmental movement was certainly not perfect, a bit too populated with spiritually confused 'wannabes', but basically benevolent in its own way. Though I was never inclined to be a joiner of formal groups and organizations, I thought of myself as generally supporting environmentalism's goals. Now I shudder to think how many of its petitions I may have signed without knowing the other side of the story.

There was a huge turnout for the meeting at the little all-purpose Civic Hall in Curlew. The place was crowded and there was a fellow video taping the event. The condescending tone the ranger's voice assumed when he responded to the local folk's questions set my hackles to bristle.

Were these hardworking people paying this man's salary to be treated like peons and listen to him talk in circles without really telling them anything? This was the land they'd lived in and loved for generations. His answers to everything seemed to depend upon yet more inaccessible studies and mysterious bureaucratic paper shuffling protocols.

If this was the agency's notion of public participation, then it certainly had come up with a style that excluded local folks by means of vagueness and evasion, if nothing else. I heard shades of Indiantown and Suedberg in the ranger's voice. His air of superiority was unsettling. I decided to ask a few questions.

Well, he didn't have that information with him, he said, must have left it back at the office. It seems he didn't have much of the information with him at all that he needed to answer my questions. It made me wonder just what he was really planning on talking about that night. But he told me - on video-tape - that if I signed in on his sign-in sheet I would get the information I needed before the public comment deadline date.

At that point, I didn't even know what a public comment date was, but I wanted that information anyway because I smelled a land grab. Hiding behind the elaborate concerns about our little old dirt roads impeding wildlife, and potential suitable habitat for lynx that might possibly be there, depending on what further studies showed, was something that didn't sound right. The area is described as pristine, and it is teaming with wildlife. But, I *had* seen some pretty heavy military traffic go up into the area these folks were talking about closing. Didn't *that* disturb wildlife?

I had no idea back then that the environmental industry had decided the solution to every question of rural ecology was essentially to remove rural people from the landscape.   The efficient mammalian predators they're so concerned about live pretty much wherever they please, with or without studies, as long as you don't shoot them. So it was with the healthy male cougar that nearly had my youngest son for lunch at age five in broad daylight, right in front of the cabin and his teenage sister. Neither the badgers that ate my chickens, the coyotes that ate my cats, or the bear that stole all the elderberries I hung out on the porch to dry seemed one bit intimidated by our human presence.

Mind you, there's plenty of wildlife for them to eat. We're busting at the seams with it around here. Right now we've got more cougar and deer than you can shake a stick at. But the cougar are attacking anything from little kids, to horses, to the dog on your front porch, simply because they can. It's not a case of people population growth around these parts, the people count is shrinking. But the cougars *do* know we no longer shoot them when they strike in our own back yards. Because of laws created by people who know nothing about the reality of living with wildlife, now we have to wait for a fish and wildlife officer to take over the situation.

All wildlife goes through population cycles, but it abounds where ranching and farming occur. The main thing is not to hunt and eat too much of it yourself when the population is on the low end of the cycle. Now getting rid of *drunken* urban hunters would help everybody's peace of mind, rural humans, wild critters and domestic animals alike. There's nothing more sickening than coming across a fat doe that some trigger-happy booze-blind fool shot and then left behind after he got a closer look at it. Their bullets flying around your house, kids, horses, livestock and dogs is obviously unacceptable, but it happens way too often.

If you're unfortunate enough to have some hunting magazine yap about what a great deer population you've got, you can expect a veritable army of fluorescent party animals with guns to swarm all over the place come deer season. That's when all the wild critters hide and folks like me get tired of uninvited guests. One year a couple of drunks rolled in late at night and set up their camp right on the side of my driveway, smack dab in front of a big no trespassing, no hunting sign. If you're looking for proof that we have a shamefully high illiteracy rate in the US, come on out and watch deer season.

And no, the mammalian predators are not impeded by dirt roads or even afraid of men with chain saws. A cougar will stalk a grown man out cutting firewood with a big, noisy chain saw, and it doesn't have a single qualm about crossing a dirt road to do so. Neither will the bear that wants to eat the apples in your yard before he snuggles up for winter hibernation. If some of the new era of conservation biologists making goofy pronouncements actually lived their whole lives with the animals they claim to know all about, they'd have a much better understanding of the circle of life.

The land grabber is another critter I know, and it was beginning to sound like saving species was more about getting people off the land than the realities of living with wildlife. That's a cruel thing to do to the very people who love wildlife the most— to pit them against each other like that.

So, I found out right after that meeting about closing roads and saving lynx what the term "public comment date" means. Seems that's your narrow little window of opportunity to submit to a government agency your written opinion of what they are proposing to do to your community. By law, they are supposed to consider your comments before making a decision to act.

At that point I also had no idea that the well considered and experienced opinion of the land's inhabitants would be overwhelmed by petitions and form letters signed by droves of misinformed city people that never even set foot in the community.

But I *was* disturbed that the information the district ranger had promised did not reach me till the day before the comment date. Some would call this an attempt to obstruct informed timely comment and public participation. What I found when I read the information is what really took the cake.

Washington State Department of Ecology had placed Lone Ranch Creek on it's 303-d list some years before. This was based on water samples that exceeded agency standards for fecal coliform, provided by Forest Service hydrology technicians. In plain language, that means the DOE was saying that Lone Ranch Creek was polluted with critter poop. Cows were being heavily implicated as the villains in the Forest Service document that lay before me. This is not only the water my kids used to play in, it is the water we often used to drink. Something seemed suspicious.

I called the Forest Service office in Republic, the county seat, for more details on this questionable looking water quality data. The fellow said they didn't have the information there, if you can imagine that, but gave me the name of the head hydrologist at the main Colville National Forest office. He would have the data I wanted.

Bert Wasson, nearing retirement, kindly provided me with copies of the data for Lone Ranch that DOE listing was based upon. To my surprise, the data, collected at two locations in each of the two years, did not even meet the procedural criteria established for the agency to list a creek. Even more interesting, the supposedly incriminating data itself looked all wrong for what the agencies and the local environmentalists were implying about cattle, and more recent data showed the creek was really in good condition.

The remarkably high fecal coliform counts obtained on both the
north and south forks of the creek in 1992 occurred at times I
knew there were no cattle located anywhere nearby. I double-
checked this with Aldeena Grumbach, Curly's wife, and their official Forest Service grazing records. It sure looked as though
someone really may have been purposely dumping cow dung in
the creek to get such data, as some folks suspected. They thought
maybe someone connected with the "Cattle Free by '93" campaign that wanted to stop all cattle grazing on the range might
have done it. But it sure wasn't the cows because they had a
solid alibi. They weren't there.

It's possible the folks who lived at the cabin before me knew
something about it. She had worked for the Forest Service. Locals report that back at that time the former district ranger allowed the local environmental group such latitude that they had a
desk right there in the Republic office.

Some Earth First! activists who had insinuated themselves into
the community were filmed on video defacing a Forest Service
office with garbage sacks full of cow dung in one of their Cattle
Free by '93 protests next door in Okanogan County. These guys
now have well-paid positions with environmental organizations. It
is people like this that began to make me feel a bit embarrassed to
have been an Evergreen student.

Earth First's tree spiking had always struck me as nothing more
than coercion with threat of violent death. This was the revolution of love that began in the sixties? I think not. It was plain and
simple terror directed against human beings. The real live working people who were supporting their families by felling trees or
running sawmills were the ones who would be injured or killed by
the spikes, not the international timber fat cats.

Now the tree spikers use cement or porcelain spikes to hide their
sabotage from woodcutters with metal detectors. Believe me, it
makes you worry when your own loved ones work in the woods
or the local lumber mill. If their saw blade hits such a hidden
spike, it can maim them for life or kill them.

You would think *some* human rights person would have paid attention. Joan Baez is apparently too busy these days singing to yuppie-offspring tree sitters to notice what's actually happening to the common working people she gained so much fame and money singing about. First it was tree spikes and blown-up logging equipment. Now it's also family ranchers in the same environmentalists' crosshairs. These guys, I have discovered, don't play nice. They will break the rules to win.

Even more curious was the 1995 water quality data. That was the year the young fellow who said he was from Fish and Wildlife asked me if he could take water samples from the creek where I had lived on the North Fork of Lone Ranch Creek. This was on private land, far below the actual National Forest entrance. Between me and the Forest entrance, there was a huge, privately owned pasture where my neighbor, Doug Grumbach, kept his valuable registered Angus cattle. You don't put that kind of livestock on the range with cattle that grazes far up in the hills.

Another call to Bert Wasson and more to the Fish and Wildlife people told me that only the Forest Service, not Fish and Wildlife, had taken water samples from the creek that year. Yet here was this Forest Service water quality data DOE used to keep the creek listed, saying the samples had been collected on National Forest land where standards are significantly stricter.

If that was really the case, then who was taking samples in the creek where I lived and what in the world did he do with them? Had that young technician really taken the samples from the creek at my place - just below my neighbor's Angus - in the hopes of catching some fecal matter with which to incriminate the range cows way up above on the National Forest?

I realized there was no shortage of zealous young environmentalists that came right out of schools like my old alma mater that want nothing more than to eliminate cattle grazing. To hear many of them talk, you would think that a cow is the devil himself. These people started out years ago with summer jobs. By now they've worked their way up the agency ladders. But I didn't want to believe that professionals would stoop so low as to cheat to prove their biases. That's not the scientific method I learned in school.

If I had known then about the procedural violations in lynx hair studies here in Washington that caused such a ruckus in the nation's capitol in 2002, I might have been a bit more wary when that young technician asked to take water samples. It seems that several government biologists involved in these lynx studies submitted hairs from captive lynx in a study that was intended to establish whether wild lynx were present in certain forests. When it all came out in the news, they said they were only testing the lab's ability to identify samples, even though their actions were prohibited by the studies' protocols. Quite a few rural folks are having trouble accepting that explanation, but environmental organizations all seem to stoutly defend these guys.

At any rate, Bert wasn't able to tell me who the long gone summer technician was. He couldn't really vouch for what the young man had or hadn't done, because, as he pointed out, he can't follow his technicians all over the Colville National Forest. But this time he said he would send me copies of the original hand written field notes and a map submitted by the technician to indicate where the samples were taken.

Well, the technician had marked the alleged location of the sampling in question with a big old "X" way above my place on the National Forest. It seemed to me that this could have hardly been an accident. The map clearly indicated the parcel where I lived, and it is clearly *not* within the National Forest. So, I checked the times the young man had recorded taking the samples at each of the two sites on each sampling excursion. Sure enough, there was not enough time for him to travel from the first location on the south fork and reach the National Forest location he had indicated on the north fork within the sampling times he had recorded.

Whether a case of sloppy record-keeping, inability to read a simple map, or deliberate falsification of data, all possible explanations are rather disturbing and unacceptable. Neither incompetence nor deceit will result in good land, water and wildlife management. This kind of behavior from management agency personnel is not what the rural people whose lives are entwined with this land deserve. Neither is this the public good that all the TV educated masses think they are getting when they cast a vote for nature.

It does look like the young Forest Service technician had falsified federal water quality data, and lied to me about who he was employed by. I never have liked a liar. What I knew I saw that day was essentially a young elitist professional who believed it was OK to cheat and lie to get families and their livestock off the land. I saw someone who thought he had a better use for the land, someone willing to lie and ruin people's lives to force his wishes on them despite the lack of substantiating science.

What I didn't know then was that a huge portion of this forest had been targeted nationally by big money environmental coalitions for Wilderness or National Monument designation for the last decade—designations that would virtually remove all humans except backpackers and various agency-approved science personnel from the land.

I gave the water quality information to the folks who run their cattle in the grazing allotments involved, to the County Commissioners, and a few other very concerned people. Interestingly enough, the Forest Service shortly after that recommended that DOE remove Lone Ranch Creek from their dirty water list. Washington Department of Ecology hasn't done that yet, last I heard.

Now there is even more evidence that cows are not polluting Lone Ranch Creek. Concerned local people decided that the ranchers and the rest of the community needed to obtain their own data, just like I had said to Curly— data they *know* has been obtained according to the rules of science.

Seed funding was provided by the Upper Columbia Resource Council for a groundbreaking DNA identified water quality testing program on local creeks listed by DOE as quality impaired. Randy Williams of the WSU ag extension gathered funding for what became the Kettle Tri-Watershed Project. DNA testing would prove with certainty just what was and wasn't polluting the waters with fecal coliform. We could pinpoint any potential problems.

With local legwork and the impeccable abilities of University of Washington DNA expert, Professor Mansour Samadpour, Lone Ranch Creek and its range cattle have been vindicated. Their poop is nothing compared to wildlife's contributions.

But deer and elk are in deep do-do, so to speak. Seems they're the biggest offenders. Next in line is wild fowl. Hmmm...deer diapers? Depends for ducks? Potty-train the coyotes?

And what are we going to do about the fish? Well, maybe they should be trained to leap out of the water into porta-potties to defecate.

One day my mom sent another news clipping from home. The state of Pennsylvania said the gypsy moth trouble was over and thirty years later it was time to flood the old farmlands at Suedberg where Grandpa Daubert's family farm was taken by the government.

'No! This is Wilderness now!' the environmentalists said. 'We have found some endangered bog turtles! You cannot flood this land!'

'Well then let us buy our land back!' the oppressed old farmers said. 'We got along just fine with turtles, they liked it on our land!'

'Oh, no!' cried the ecologists, 'You cannot have this land. Wilderness is sacred to us, it cannot be touched by man!'

I was inspired to write a little pamphlet about the anti-Indian, anti-human wilderness movement and handed it out at the County Fair. Pretty soon, out of the blue, I got a call from a 'Kim'(first name only), the communications director of the Wildlands Project. He just wanted to be dumbfounded that an indigenous person, who had attended Evergreen to boot, and lived a simple life, could think the way I do.

Those guys just don't seem to get it that practically worshipping the *idea* of wilderness at a distance, which is what they want us to do, is not the same as loving Mother Earth enough to be able to live *with* her respectfully. These folks suffer from a spiritual sickness of their own in which they believe that humans essentially cannot live in harmony with the land. Nothing is ever pure enough for them. They remind me of Lady Macbeth and the bloody spot she tried so frantically to remove.

I asked 'Kim' if he thought all those rich transnational corporations and foundations would keep giving the Wildlands Project and wilderness coalitions money after they ran all the 'common people' and their small natural resource businesses off the land. He didn't have an answer, but he sent me a slick Wildlands Project information packet. He was certain I'd been misinformed and could maybe still be made to see the light.

He obviously didn't begin to fathom how many centuries of resistance to land grabbers are in my genes. These folks had said that 50% to 95% of the whole country must be wilderness virtually untouched by humans. That seems a bit much, and the methods of achieving it a gross violation of human rights.

In February 2000, the US House Resources subcommittee on Forests and Forest Health asked me to testify about what effect the faraway wealthy funders of modern environmentalism have had in Ferry County. Four minutes were allotted to talk about what I had learned from my research and from residents throughout the county. But that was apparently enough time to make some people very angry.

My introduction stated I was, at the time, chair of the Upper Columbia Resource Council. Quite intentionally, I did not mention my own ethnic identity, just to be certain no one got the notion I was speaking for any tribe whatsoever. I even mentioned that my mother's people were removed from Indiantown Gap, which is in Pennsylvania. My actual testimony can be verified in the Congressional Record.

Despite these facts, *someone* spread false accusations clear across the country, to certain activists in Ferry County. *Someone* said I claimed to represent the Colville Confederated Tribes. Whether it was an intentional lie, or a reporter who initially made false assumptions, I may never know for sure, but what followed wasn't pretty. When I say land-based communities are besieged by people with a divide and conquer mentality willing to lie and cheat to win, I know whereof I speak.

For the sake of clarity, I emphasize, I am not a Colville. I do not live on the Colville Reservation. I live on the north half of Ferry County. That being said—that Spring, anti-grazing proponents tried to end cattle grazing permits to non-Indian ranchers and raise grazing fees for tribal members on the Colville Reservation, and make the reservation closed range only. The Colville tribal membership, however, advised the tribal council against all three actions by a 2/3 majority.

Removing livestock grazing families from "public" land has been a goal of wilderness and deep ecology activists for many years. Now the deep ecologists are trying to drum up public support for a one-time federal buyout of 25,000 Western grazing permits. Anyone familiar with the fiasco of federal tribal termination policy and its one-time buyouts should already be the wiser.

That small town meeting in Curlew about closing off our access to the woods led me to discoveries that pulled me out of the woods to call attention to injustices that are being widely ignored. These injustices are funded and directed by the same old land grabbing hand that caused centuries of human misery. It is a war that not only never ended, it has expanded.

This work hasn't been a "bed of roses". I have received hate mail and warnings that my reputation has been intentionally smeared to cut me off from my own culture. I've been cursed, maliciously slandered, publicly libeled and ridiculed. My life and safety have been threatened. I have been told that I will not be safe at certain locations and events throughout the country. The security of my family's home has been violated. The vehicles I drive my children and grandchild in have been tampered with.

What kind of people believe they have the right - or need - to threaten one tiny little woman? Terrorize her children? Threaten a mother and grandmother whose conscience can not justify silence?

I was raised in a culture that was nearly destroyed by the desperate silence imposed by vicious oppression. My elders' long and painful imprisonment in that silence purchased our survival. They are my heroes. Grandma Lillian chose the time to break that silence. Again, she is my hero.

In the words of Martin Luther King, Jr. — "There comes a time when silence is betrayal."

Part Two

The Second Wave of Manifest Destiny

But then came the men in their boats and they brought us gifts. They asked for just a little land and we foolishly gave it to them. Then, when they asked us for more land and we would not give it to them, they asked us to sell it to them and because they had goods that were new and powerful to us, we sold them some. Then they asked us for more land and when we would not give it or sell it, they took it from us and we talked and talked and always it was we who gave in and signed a new treaty and took gifts for what was taken, but the gifts were cheap and worthless and lasted but a day, while the land lasts forever.

Sconondoa, Oneida

"Indian Policy" has now been brought down upon the American people, and the American people are the new Indians of the 21st Century.

Russell Means, Lakota

- Chapter Five -

Manifest Destiny, Plutocracy, and Cultural Cleansing

The dominant political-economic figures who engineered removal of America's first inhabitants from the landscape generally excused their actions with the Doctrine of Manifest Destiny. Similar to the earlier papal Doctrine of Discovery, this doctrine, too, was contrived to make conquest of indigenous peoples and land grabs sound righteous. While the Doctrine of Manifest Destiny was initially also based on the notion of right to conquer in the name of religion, it eventually became synonymous with a somewhat less religious but more nationalistic and industrialist sense of perceived destiny.

In essence, the doctrine claims that someone who has a higher purpose for the land than those who currently live on it, also has the right, the destiny and the duty to take that land.

Conversely, the current occupants purportedly lose their rights because their purpose for the land is deemed lower, perhaps even unholy. The doctrine says this is all made obvious - made manifest - by the fact that the taker has a higher purpose. It further claims that because this higher purpose must be fulfilled, the taker must use whatever means necessary to take the land from its occupants.

Thus the conqueror claims it is his manifest destiny to take the land. Human decency itself should condemn this concept and rethink—who *really* has the right to make such decisions?

However, this manifest destiny belief *is* how violent, genocidal conquest of the sovereign Indian nations was excused. With this mindset, government then strung a trail of Indian treaties across the continent. The treaties promised specific land, water and resources to the tribes. Since this was all done with the manifest destiny attitude as its basis, it is no surprise that after the tribes were conquered, government's promises to them were not upheld.

The rich and powerful public and private figures who most influenced government decisions had this manifest destiny attitude. American politics became polluted by the influence of plutocrats - rich people who rule by the might of their wealth - who also believed it was their manifest destiny to do so. Thus the doctrine's attitude, combined with plutocratic influence, became embedded in government policy making.

Before long, the notion of manifest destiny was not limited strictly to the conquest of Indian nations. In 1845, the Democratic Review boldly declared: "Texas has been absorbed into the Union in the inevitable fulfillment of the general law which is rolling our population westward....It was disintegrated from Mexico in the natural course of events, by a process perfectly legitimate on its own part, blameless on ours....(its) incorporation into the Union was not only inevitable, but the most natural, right and proper thing in the world....California will, probably, next fall away....Imbecile and distracted, Mexico never can exert any real governmental authority over such a country....The Anglo-Saxon foot is already on its borders." By the mid-1800's, then, the US manifest destiny attitude was already expanding beyond conquest of Indians.

As each Indian nation was conquered, government proceeded to string yet another network of promises of land, water and resources across the land. These promises were made to the average citizen in order to resettle the land, in the form of land grants, land patents, water rights, and so on. Such citizens were generally more easily controlled by government than the Indian.

This resettlement effectively helped plutocratic forces within government to fulfill their own purpose for the land. The elite class pushed the notion of manifest destiny to the public in the newspapers, giving the average white citizen the idea that he, too, had a manifest destiny in common with the elite. Yet the actual history of the period and later developments make it evident that the plutocratic forces agreed to allow the general public the opportunity to own land because it suited their own financial and political goals at the time.

This second set of government promises to U.S. citizens often overlap with previous treaty promises to Indian tribes. Promising the same item to two different parties is obviously wrong and inevitably causes conflict. Adding to these conflicts, some tribes were also forced to give up their reservation lands.

In 1887, the Dawes (General Allotment) Act was celebrated by the power elite within government. Allotment policy was designed to put yet more Indian land into non-Indian citizens' hands. In *The Crucible of American Indian Identity,* Cherokee professor Ward Churchill writes: "Allotment and the broader assimilation policy of which it was part had truly proven themselves to be, in the words of Indian Commissioner Francis E. Leupp, 'a mighty pulverizing engine for breaking up the tribal mass.'"

And in his own autobiography, what did Teddy Roosevelt say about Indian affairs and Leupp? "In connection with the Indians, by the way, it was again and again necessary to assert the position of the President as steward of the whole people. I had a capital Indian Commissioner, Francis E. Leupp. I found that I could rely on his judgment not to get me into fights that were unnecessary, and therefore I always backed him to the limit when he told me that a fight was necessary."

Let's be clear about this: Teddy saw Indian Commissioner Leupp's guidance - along with the genocidal allotment and assimilation policies - as essential to preventing *Indian* concerns from impeding his stewardship of the *whole* people. In other words, he was saying that public interest trumped government's promises in Indian treaties. This is a precedent that the Indian nations would do well to remember.

But, let's also remember that Teddy Roosevelt was the father of the federal nature conservation program that forced so many unwilling non-Indian people to sell their lands to establish the National Parks System. So government also maintains that public interest trumps government's promises to non-Indian citizens. Any government promise can be broken, government says, in the name, ironically, of public good.

The father of American federal conservation programs was certainly complicit with genocide of Indians. Yet, by his time, we can also see that the plutocratic manifest destiny mindset already had not only Indian and Mexican land in its crosshairs, but everyday white citizens' land, as well.

Following the blow dealt the tribes by allotment and assimilation policy came termination policy. With termination, government systematically declared that certain federally recognized tribes were, suddenly, not tribes. Government then proceeded to divest these newly 'non-existent' tribes of their lands, putting the lands into private citizens' or government agency hands.

Ward Churchill points out that the federal government only re-examined this policy when it realized that Indian reservation lands contained a wealth of mineral and energy resources. Unwilling to lose the control of these resources its 'trust' authority over Indian lands gave it, government refrained from putting any more such mineral, gas and oil rich lands into private citizen's hands through tribal termination.

Today, a number of terminated tribes have rightly regained their federal recognition, and so, any treaties made with them are once again legally positioned so that they must be honored by government.

Clearly, a massive tangle of conflicting government promises for land, water and natural resources was left in the wake of the first wave of manifest destiny that roared across the continent. Despite the fact that these conflicts are not nearly all resolved, in the late 20th Century government began to make sweeping laws intended to protect our environment. As court decisions mount up, we now find these new environmental laws often conflict with government's previous promises of land, water, and resources to

Indians and non-Indians. Government's tangle of conflicting promises thus has become even more frustrating for the public to resolve.

As we enter the 21st Century, evidence suggests that the same old bane of the Indian nations, the Doctrine of Manifest Destiny, not only persists but has greatly expanded the populations in its scope. The doctrine has been taken up by surprising new bedfellows who - whether in word or action - advocate removal of people from the land. The problem now, as in the past, is—who really has the right to make such decisions?

*****

The identity of manifest destiny's new bedfellows may shock those yet unwashed by today's rural reality. However, the creeping socioeconomic impoverishment that is gutting rural American landscapes will itself, by and by, identify them as the lapdog agents of a perennial plutocratic elite. The agents' faithful followers, it will be found, have been incredibly deceived, their best intentions shamelessly misused.

Unlike the familiar old promoters of manifest destiny, its new agents make a great show of condemning past and present violations of Indian rights. They even 'borrow' Indian religion, spiritual symbols and treaty rights to promote their presumed higher purpose for the land. In fact, they often behave as though the Indian is their mascot.

But manifest destiny's 'friendly' new agents have some dirty little secrets. Beneath their polished façade, elitism and the same old racism are revealed.

These new 'friends' proclaim their respect for tribal sovereignty with one face, yet with another they oppose tribal governments' natural resource use decisions whenever they don't agree. They have a record of fighting tribes who try to recover even small portions of their lost lands because they don't want the tribes to manage or harvest the natural resources those lands contain.

What the doctrine's newest agents are really saying is, "We will help you get your treaty-promised natural resources when it pleases us. But if we don't approve of how you use them, we will have to fight you. You are not wise enough to make your own decisions."

Opposition to indigenous people's hunting rights takes this ugly attitude a step further. For example, those who fight against the Makah traditional whale hunt don't just insult Indian intelligence and tradition. They also reveal violent racist attitudes: Bumper stickers say, "Save a whale, harpoon a Makah". Anti-whaling boats attempt to physically interfere with the hunt, endangering Makah whalers on the water. Whalers receive death threats.

The venom anti-whalers spew at Indians are an ironic twist on L. Frank Baum's racist attitude. Baum should be more remembered for his anti-Indian rhetoric than authoring *The Wizard of Oz*.

Baum's news weekly, the Saturday Pioneer, in December 1890 said— "the nobility of the Redskin is extinguished, and what few are left are a pack of whining curs who lick the hand that smites them. The Whites, by law of conquest, by justice of civilization, are masters of the American continent, and the best safety of the frontier settlements will be secured by the total annihilation of the few remaining Indians. Why not annihilation? Their glory has fled, their spirit broken, their manhood effaced: better that they die than live the miserable wretches that they are."

Animal rights and deep ecology activists crying 'death' to Makah whalers war on Indian culture, using similar violent, genocidal rhetoric. While Baum declared that Indian men no longer free to roam and hunt had lost their manhood, the anti-whalers insult Makah manhood for doing precisely that hunt tradition. Like Baum, they assume their notion of civilization gives them the right to impose their own genocidal vision on Indian people. In the case of deep ecologists, wilderness activists and animal rightists, their vision is a fantasy world that is as bizarre and false as the Land of Oz.

Manifest destiny's newest adherents are anxious to take water from agriculture and halt logging. Their claim is this will restore fish populations and treaty guaranteed fish harvests. Yet they campaign to limit fish catches in many ways and destroy hatcheries and hatchery-born fish that many tribes value.

Lest anyone doubt the value hatcheries can hold for the tribes, in May 2000, Rocky Barker wrote— "Chuck Axtell's ancient song rang through the Johnson Creek canyon, a prayer of strength for thousands of 4-inch chinook salmon starting their 800-mile journey to the Pacific....The endangered chinook salmon, raised in the McCall National Hatchery, were returned to the native water of their parents by a fisheries team of the Nez Perce Tribe. Axtell's blessing was an expression of hope these fish will become a lifeline that preserves the unique characteristics that keep salmon returning to Johnson Creek and Idaho." *(Prayers Offered Salmon Before Run to Pacific*, Idaho Statesman)

The new self-proclaimed 'friends of the Indian' also fail to inform the urban voter that many Indian families have been in farming, ranching and timber for generations and want to pass this self-reliant life on the land to their children. These livelihoods have enabled Indian families to escape poverty and welfarization. Yet, when these natural resource producers *are* begrudgingly acknowledged, they are often labeled as ignorant victims of big industry or even crooked 'good old boys'.

In a few rare instances associated with opposition to mining, a weak display of support is made by some for a few Indian livestock grazers. Yet manifest destiny's new agents pursue national campaigns to end logging *and* livestock grazing on all 'public' lands. In reality, these are state and federally managed lands on which many Indian people work. These campaigns promote buyout schemes to remove grazers from 'public' lands that will ultimately prove no better than the old termination schemes.

It is particularly revealing that the apparent new agents of manifest destiny show no concern whatsoever for the millions of unrecognized Indians whose rights are lost in a sea of government paperwork.

These Indian people have been systematically disenfranchised by federal policies for two centuries in order to increase the federal estate. Yet the new 'friends of the Indian' turn a blind eye to these injustices. Such is the nature of manifest destiny.

So, too, the essential human rights of non-Indian inhabitants of the land are ignored and violated. Local sovereignty is a term that manifest destiny's newest agents don't even bother to apply to non-Indians. Freedom for people of the land, freedom from centralized government control, is simply not in their political vocabulary.

Interviewed by Linda Brookover in a piece titled *The Existential Indian*, Russell Means - a leader in the American Indian Movement since its inception - stresses that living with the land requires freedom. Brookover asks about the Indian outlook on the environment, but Means says he doesn't want to talk about it. "You can't talk about the environment" and other freedom issues, he says, "unless you have a free society based upon the integrity of the individual. If you have a responsible society, these other issues will not come up in a responsible society, and that is what freedom is all about."

Means sees a bigger picture of the American landscape—" 'Indian Policy' has now been brought down upon the American people, and the American people are the new Indians of the 21st Century. Getting rid of [the] family farmer and the family rancher, subsidizing the farms and getting them to become dependent on the government, that's 'Indian Policy'." He also concludes that dependence on centralized government goes hand-in-hand with corporate dependence. In other words, Means paints a picture of modern manifest destiny, plutocracy and cultural oppression, or cultural cleansing.

The federal 'Indian policy' of replacing freedom with centralized government control is a product of the manifest destiny mindset. It is, indeed, now forced upon Indian *and* non-Indian within the rural landscape by a variety of social, economic, political and regulatory pressures. These pressures often strain and damage the social and economic fabric and well-being of land-based communities. Against this stressful backdrop, it is no wonder that governments' overlapping promises to Indian and non-Indian people are causing conflicts that make their way into the headlines every day.

There's an old saying that you can't always believe what people say, but you can always believe what they do. My own ancestral history showed me this certainly applies to anyone who thinks they have a better use for your land than how you use it. Thus we can identify manifest destiny's surprising new bedfellows.

As Chief Ray Yowell of the Western Shoshone National Council says: "First, they stuck us out on these remote reservations, where it's almost impossible to make a living…And then they restrict the land use. These environmentalists come out here from the cities and tell us how to care for the land."

For those who think only of infamous scoundrels like Andrew Jackson, George Armstrong Custer, J. P. Morgan and crooked BIA attorneys as the agents of manifest destiny, identifying the environmental industry as a culprit is a bit of a shock. Yes, I did say "the environmental *industry*". The old environmental *movement* is essentially dead.

*****

The old environmental movement that intended to safeguard this earthly habitat for humanity died from internal injuries—entangling alliances, ambitious vanity, spiritual confusion and hypocrisy. It betrayed both the urban laborer and the people of the rural landscape. It took Mother Earth's name in vain and presumed its own manifest destiny as the new *big* industry claiming a higher purpose for the land   a billion dollar industry investing in and financed by big industry fortunes.

In his Z Magazine piece titled *Questioning Official Environmentalism,* Goddard faculty member and environmental writer Brian Tokar observes: "The corporate co-optation of Earth Day, an idea that provoked intense controversy in 1990, and brought hundreds of people to demonstrate on Wall Street, had become conventional wisdom by mid-decade."

A few environmentalists like Tokar do rail against the environmental industry's big money corruption. But it hasn't made any real difference. Granted, the old movement's limbs are still twitching. Yet its soul was sold to wealthy masters long ago. Now it perversely marches on like an army of living dead. But the heart and humanity of the movement is most assuredly dead, and it is dragging the rest of us along to its ignominious grave.

Environmental leadership has become unduly impressed with itself. They are like a band of foolish, conceited, little emperors who wear no clothes—all rushing to the same global industrialist foundation wealth and tax enriched pork barrel trough they pretend to condemn and, at the same time, covet with great relish.

Today environmental leadership embraces the same fatal temptations and addictions that gained control of other social change movements first born from the grassroots in the twentieth century. The emergence of these popular movements once promised to revolutionize the whole welfare of humanity. But their leaders soon abandoned the ideal of human rights in exchange for favor and funding from the entrenched old masters of political-economic power.

Whether left or right oriented matters not, really. The self-deluded who fancy themselves important environmental figures are all trained to eat from the master's hand, so to speak. They claim their movement is democratic, but it has become the same old plutocracy in action.

Environmental leadership betrays and misuses the best intentions of their grassroots following. The high dollar campaigns of modern popular environmentalism are molded, and its grassroots following is mobilized, to conform with the aims and approval of those who provide a winning war chest. Grassroots membership dues are nothing compared to staggering sums of corporate and private foundation grant money. These grants are what steer the environmental industry.

It's called 'accountability' in 'venture philanthropy'. These are rather sanitary words that mask the actual nature of grant giving and plutocracy. In *American Foundations*, pro-environment author Mark Dowie's research finds that over $420 billion dollars worth of philanthropic foundations exercise "power far beyond their wealth". He describes "indisputably plutocratic" foundations that are staffed by people "bent on developing an agenda for the nation".

Dowie reports that their "influence derives directly from the pro-active nature of their grantmaking and their methods of leveraging money". A number of current books on foundations stress that their giving is now pro-active and issue-oriented. In plain English, these foundations maximize their control on the nation, and on our lives, by coordinating and prescribing how the money they give will be used and by demanding the results they want. Future grants are given only to those who produce the result the wealthy grantmakers desire.

Now we begin to understand the stunning wealth and plutocratic mindset that fund and direct environmental campaigns through the Environmental Grantmakers Association (EGA). Association membership consists of up to 200 foundations, trusts and endowments, most formed from the wealth of various industry empires, which can coordinate their environmental 'venture philanthropy' to maximize 'accountability' and 'solid returns'. The EGA's website states:

"In 1987, a group of environmental grantmakers met in Washington, D.C. to discuss common interests and to learn about each other's specific programs. As a result of the enthusiasm generated at this meeting, plans were made for future meetings, grants lists exchanged, and a 'directory' of foundation program interests was published. Subsequent meetings have reaffirmed this interest for increased communication among grantmakers through the EGA."

The Environmental Grantmakers Association's purposes listed on its website include: "To facilitate communication, foster cooperation, and develop collaboration among active and potential members...To provide the means by which members can improve their effectiveness as grantmakers...To communicate grantmaker interests and activities to grantseekers and other interested parties." It bears repeating, in plain English—these foundations maximize their control on the nation, and on our lives, by prescribing and coordinating how the money they give will be used and by demanding the results they want. 'Strings' are attached to their gifts.

Lest we doubt Dowie's assessment of big money foundations' power over our lives, *Inside American Philanthropy: The Drama of Donorship*, by Waldemar Nielsen, observes: "Not bound by voters, shareholders, or customers - and with only featherlight oversight by government - they couldn't possibly be allowed to exist with such potential power and such utter freedom of action in a democratic society. But they do."

It would be wise, then, to apply Mark Dowie's caution about these "indisputably plutocratic" donors to the motives and influence of the Environmental Grantmakers Association's fabulously wealthy membership. He writes: "At the turn of a new century - and a new millennium - it is time for our allegedly open society to ask whether placing so much power, covert or overt, at the disposal of an existentially bewildered, nondemocratic institution is an entirely wholesome development."

With this in mind, further statements on the EGA website should cause all of us a good bit of concern. Under "EGA Workings Groups" it says EGA members "may organize or participate in working groups to discuss issues of common interest, hold briefings, and produce reports."

Current working groups focus on agriculture, the economy, transportation, the West, the Great Lakes, resource recovery, land use, growth management, and minorities. Bear in mind, the members of these working groups are wealthy industry-enriched foundations, not the average citizen, and certainly not the average minority citizen.

Under "Member-Initiated Projects" the website says, "EGA members are invited and encouraged to initiate regional conferences, briefing packets on timely issues, and oral funder briefings. The oral briefings serve primarily as opportunities for colleagues to participate in small, interactive discussions with speakers who have interesting ideas and perspectives. The briefing packets are more in-depth studies and have included such topics as trade and environment, population and environment, and reauthoritzation of environmental legislation."

Here are the social and economic elite, working together to exert maximum influence on virtually every aspect of our lives. From 'minorities and the environment' to environmental legislation, these privileged few use their money to control what we think and do. They organize, plan and act to control how we use our land, water and minerals, how we grow our food, what we eat, where we live, how we live, how we travel and how many of us will be doing all of this.

In *Questioning Official Environmentalism,* Brian Tokar refers to *The Multinational Monitor's* findings of multinational corporate influence on environmentalism. It referred to 23 directors or council members of the Audubon Society, Natural Resource Defense Council, Wilderness Society, World Resources Institute, and World Wildlife Fund. These 23 environmental movement leaders were also connected to 19 different corporations that were all named in an up-to-date survey of the 500 worst polluters of the environment. This is today's environmental leadership.

Tokar also reports, "Journalist Mark Dowie discovered that of the approximately $3 billion contributed to environmental advocates each year, the 25 largest organizations get 70 percent, while the remaining share is divided among some 10,000 smaller, more local groups."

According to Dowie's figures, environmentalism is clearly not a grassroots movement anymore. That's an average of *$84 million per year* for the top dogs, and a mere annual average of $90 *thousand* for the smaller groups that must carry out the big dogs' campaigns on the local level or else receive no further funding.

Bear in mind, there is *no* big foundation funding for little environmental groups who do not produce the funders' desired results.

The ultimate control of multinational industrial wealth and the Environmental Grantmakers Association over environmentalism in America is profoundly obvious. Thus the term *environmental industry* is right on target.

Back in 1992, at EGA's annual retreat - "Environmental Legislation" session - Anne Fitzgerald asked whether these funders detected "a resistance in the larger organizations to becoming grant driven"—

Chuck Clusen, American Conservation Association: "...There's definitely a feeling on the part of the not-for-profit organizations that in cases of some of the campaigns like the Ancient Forests Campaign that they resent funders, not just picking the issues, but also being directive in the sense of the kind of campaign, the strategy, the style, and so on....I look at it as, if they're not going to do it on their own, thank God funders are forcing them to start doing it...."

Donald Ross, Rockefeller Family Fund: ".... I think funders have a major role to play. And I know there are resentments in the community towards funders doing that. And, too bad. We're players, they're players....I think the fundamental effort that has to be made is a reorganization of the movement....I think we have to begin to look much more at a task force approach on major issues that is able to pool. And the funders can drive that....And I think there isn't one of them, even the biggest, National Wildlife, or Audubon or Sierra Club, that has the capacity to wage full scale battles on major issues by themselves....I think it can be, where funders can play a real role is helping, is using the money to drive, to create ad hoc efforts in many cases that will have a litigation component coming from one group, a lobbying component coming from another group, a grass roots organizing component coming from yet a third group with a structure that enables them to function well."

These statements clearly reveal that the wealthy elite who fund environmentalism very intentionally pick the issues and drive the campaigns, commandeering even the grassroots groups to do their bidding. They say that the environmental movement is incapable of doing this itself. Yet, this is obviously the same old plutocratic self-interest speaking.

Not only do environmental organizations recognize this plutocratic control, but they also recognize that EGA funding serves to deflect environmentalism's campaigns away from real life corporate polluters.

In *The Dilemmas of Foundation-Backed Activism*, a piece written for Earth Island Institute by Aaron G. Lehmer, it is revealed that, indeed, big environmental organizations run their campaigns to fit with the agendas of the foundations that fund them. Further, Lehmer summarizes Oregon-based environmental activist, Jim Britell's remarks, saying that funding "tends to be for 'name-it-and-save-it' projects that rarely, if ever, take on the corporations that are causing the problems in the first place. If you want to do grassroots organizing around problems like corporate crime or corporations' central role in environmental destruction, it's almost impossible to get foundation funding, he says."

Knowing this, did environmental leadership - from the grassroots to the national and international level - then commit to stick to the movement's original principles? Did they reject this plutocratic leadership, its money and control? No. They betrayed those principles and became the plutocrat-controlled environmental *industry*. Under this leadership, they then betrayed the urban labor force, small business, and land-based rural communities—the very same masses they once proclaimed they would save from plutocratic corporate rule.

An unflinching assessment of the environmental industry leads to only one disconcerting conclusion— *The fox guards the hen house, and blames the chickens for his thieving. It is plutocracy in action. And it reeks of the manifest destiny attitude.*

*****

Centralized government's power over land use and acquisition has been astoundingly abused. It is too easily corrupted by the influence of great wealth over public opinion and legislation. This has

been the agonizing experience of the Indian nations and many
non-Indian rural communities throughout U.S. history.

Indeed, our history presents a parade of shameless figures who
presumed to have better use for rural peoples' lands and assumed
the authority to take it. The infamous Andrew Jackson - who's
cruelty to the Lenape and the Cherokee is well-known - is a prime
example. With all too much ease these influential figures turn
public opinion and even natural allies against the inhabitants of the
coveted landscape. Such is the nature of manifest destiny.

Look from the original conquest of Indian lands, to the lands taken
from Indian and non-Indian communities by eminent domain and
condemnation for New Deal projects and the National Parks system. Look from the Oklahoma oil lynchings and Indian allotment,
assimilation and termination policies, to the millions of acres now
consumed in the name of species protection and ecosystem health.
The peoples who were dispossessed of their lands were characterized by the takers as 'willing sellers'. Even if it took military
force to convince them to 'sell'.

The Indian nations' resistance, as a whole, to this manifest destiny
mindset is legendary throughout the world. Less known is the
resistance of men like Robert Via to the cultural genocide and
despicable land acquisition tactics used to establish the National
Parks in America.

Via, too, put up a legendary fight - against government taking his
family's farm and against destruction of the mountain people of
Sugar Hollow in the Blue Ridge Mountains of Virginia - when
Shenandoah National Park was established.

The Blue Ridge Mountains' mixed communities of Indians and
white settler descendants were indeed a unique culture. This is
were bluegrass music was born. Robert Via's parents, Christo-
pher and Malinda, had built up a very successful apple orchard
there in Sugar Hollow, a business that supplied work for many
mountain people. In the 1920's, when big businesses like Sinclair
Oil and Allied Chemical, along with government men, started promoting the Park as a cure for Virginia's Depression era woes,

mountain people became yet another target for cultural genocide.

The mountain people - some derisively call them "hillbillies" - had always been looked down upon and demonized by the city folk who feared them. The wealthy Park supporters dared to imply they were really doing the mountain people a favor by taking their land and ending their way of life. The urbanized masses could then feel righteous about wiping out the Shenandoah's mountain people who wanted only to love the land and live their lives in peace. Does this have a familiar ring?

Robert Via put up a long and bitter battle against this unconstitutional government taking and condemnation of family farms and mountain homes, through the Virginia courts and all the way to the US Supreme Court. In the midst of this fight, in 1927, he found it necessary to move his family to another farm, at the base of the Blue Mountain on lower Manada Creek near Hershey, Pennsylvania. That's how his son Chris came to be my grandfather.

But in 1935, the fight was over. Astoundingly, the US Supreme Court decided in favor of the land grabbers. Robert Via's determination to save Sugar Hollow proved no match for government deceit and dirty dealing. He never cashed the check the government issued for the land that he never wanted to sell. He did not consider it even remotely a just compensation for taking his family's home nor for the destruction of Sugar Hollow's culture.

The reality is that rural peoples throughout human history have never wanted to part with their lands. The 'willing seller' myth has always been a lie, just as the Doctrine of Manifest Destiny is a lie. These lies are contrived and forced upon rural people to make the ugly realities of land grabbing seem more acceptable.

Today the environmental industry and its elite backers are solidly entrenched within private and government establishment sectors. They issue the same haughty decrees one would expect of privileged people with manifest destiny mind-sets. Funding its own scientific justification, this multi-billion dollar industry decrees what must be done, claiming this is for the higher purpose of preserving the earth itself.

When Congress does not do as the plutocratic environmental industry desires, the industry takes matters into it own hands. For instance, Pew Charitable Trusts, big environmental groups and leading foundations formed the Northern Forest Alliance to protect the northern forests of New York and New England in the manner they saw fit. Smaller grant-dependent environmental groups simply had to fall in line, and did.

Philadelphia Inquirer investigative journalist Stephan Salisbury reports that Pew "created and funded dozens of programs and independent organizations to carry out agendas determined by the foundation and its consultants. It has promoted its own causes, pursued its own initiatives, bankrolled its own research and imposed its own order." The Northern Forest Alliance thus embarked on an aggressive campaign to acquire vast areas of forest land in the Northeastern states from private citizens.

The plutocratic elite do not stop at simply controlling what environmental groups do, they also control the science that is used to manage the environment. Let's have a look at another Pew program, the Pew Fellows in Conservation and the Environment.

In 1988, Pew began to award ten three-year $150,000 fellowships to scientists each year. Pew claims it established this $1.5 million per year program to "identify and support a new generation of scholar-scientists who would apply their special knowledge and skills directly to pressing environmental problems." However, Pew then altered its definition of recipients to "outstanding scientists, researchers and conservation activists." Apparently the goal of Pew's science fellowships program can't be met by awarding money only to bona fide scientists. This change enabled Pew to award more and more fellowships to non-scientist environmental activists.

Candidates apply for Pew fellowships only *after* they are nominated by a group of 37 "leaders in the conservation field" who nominate two candidates each. The group includes many people from organizations that receive Pew grants, and are, therefore, in sync with Pew's agenda. Nominators are from heavyweight groups like Environmental Defense, National Audubon Society, Natural

Resources Defense Council, Worldwatch Institute, and World Wildlife Foundation.

A sample of recent Pew fellows include: Michael Bean and David Wilcove (Environmental Defense), Johanna Wald (Natural Resources Defense Council), Victor Sher (Sierra Club Legal Defense Fund), Carl Safina (National Audubon Society) and Reed Noss.

Noss initiated the Wildlands Project with Earth First! founder Dave Foreman. The Wildlands Project is an ambitious program with a network of cooperator groups throughout the entire country. Here in Ferry County, WA, for example, Kettle Range Conservation Group is a Wildlands Project cooperator. The Project's goal is to map and convert vast regions of the US to wilderness uninhabited by humans and untouched by human activity. At its outset, Noss said that 50% of the US land mass should be made wilderness immediately, and suggested that 95% should eventually be made wilderness.

The land acquisition goals and human rights violations implicit in this massive wilderness plan are mind-boggling. Yet Noss is the kind of anti-human "scientist" plutocratic forces like Pew choose to "apply their special knowledge and skills directly to pressing environmental problems".

With this kind of direction, like a self-possessed ogre, the environmental industry then aggressively demands and forces the transfer of ownership or management of land and water into the hands of a faraway, centralized bureaucracy. That bureaucracy is populated with all too many like-thinking ogres. Government then uses anti-human 'science' and abuses public interest rationale to justify breaking its promises. Thus it tramples non-Indian and Indian local sovereignty alike.

At this point, Winona LaDuke's remarks about the relationship of local land control to poverty, quoted in the preface, bears repeating. "Indian people are poor because of structural poverty. Structural poverty means you don't actually control your land, your economy." This need for local control of the land to assure socioeconomic health, and the poverty that loss of control produces, applies to both Indian and non-Indian land-based communities. In terms of control over land use, the sovereignty tribes and non-Indian land-based communities need is very similar.

*****

Tribal governments often put up more resistance to remote centralized government control than other local governments. However, in *The Owl, the Indian, the Feminist, and the Brother: Environmentalism Encounters the Social Justice Movement*, Peter M. Manus appears to celebrate bureaucratic resourcefulness in getting around sovereignty disputes with Indian people.

Manus writes that "some states have learned to avoid the sovereignty tinderbox by scrapping attempts to regulate tribes with state law". Instead, he says, "these states enter into cooperative agreements in which tribes voluntarily agree to adopt the state's regulatory standards". This gives the appearance of local control. Such agreements are often entangled with government funding.

Resistant non-Indian local governments are sometimes dealt with similarly. Thus centralized government strings a tangled trail of "Memorandums of Agreement", "Memorandums of Understanding" and "Cooperative Agreements" across Indian and non-Indian land. These agreements tend to blur jurisdiction and ultimately diminish local sovereignty. Once centralized government has a foot in the door, further loss of local control, often tied to government funding, follows. Local control crumbles like a house of cards.

Unfortunately for the rural people already entangled in government's conflicting promises of land and water rights, the distant bureaucracy seeking to diminish local sovereignty has no familiar love for the land or its people. It fails repeatedly to protect them.

In addition to massive funds that already exist for centralized government land acquisition, more land acquisition programs like the controversial CARA (Conservation and Reinvestment Act) continue to be created. Even the well-heeled National Rifle Association supported CARA along with a coalition of big name environmental organizations known as CARE that promotes the acquisition and establishment of more wildlife preserves.

As the environmental industry pushes more and more land into centralized government control or ownership, the social and economic security of land-based communities is further harmed. This is what loss of sovereignty on the local level inevitably produces.

Throughout this process, the environmental industry handily manages to acquire a big chunk of the land for itself, often in partnership with globalizing industries. The Nature Conservancy (TNC) is reportedly one of the largest land owners and managers around, with management and research contracts even for federal land. It is also infamous for acquiring land at cut rate prices from rural owners in the name of preservation and then reselling it to government and private interests at a tidy profit. So, we might wonder if TNC got where it is today by opposing big industry.

Hardly. Astoundingly, TNC became a land and natural resource empire with a lot of help from an eye-popping list of industry titans and corporate foundations. A sampling of these contributors to TNC's empire include: Amoco, Arco, Chevron, Mobil, Phillips, Texaco, Weyerhauser, Georgia-Pacific, Kellogg, H.J. Heinz, Monsanto, Caterpillar, John Deere, Dow Chemical, Eli Lilly, Rockwell International, Boeing-McDonnell, Ford Motor, Chrysler, Merrill Lynch, BankBoston, BankAmerica, Citicorp, Scottish Power's PacifiCorp...and the disgraced energy giant, Enron. To name a few. *And* the U.S. government.

We don't really *know* how many of our federal tax dollars are given to the environmental industry. While there are over 24 different federal sources of these grants, no government agency tracks the total dollars, how they are spent, or what taxpayers get for their dollars. Critics express concern that tax dollars go to groups who fight the same agencies that granted the dollars. The Spokane, WA-based Lands Council's receipt of Forest Service moneys is an example.

Sacramento Bee staff writer Tom Knudson reports the amount is "substantial and growing." He says over half the money is used for land purchase, and restoration or protection of land and species. Whether this includes land purchase from less-than-willing sellers or money used to file lawsuits against landowners or government to change land use, we're not told. Knudson does indicate that a variety of federal records reveal our tax dollars do get spent on some lobbying, advocacy, and funding "government adversaries". Thus the critics' concerns are not unfounded. "A 1998 federal audit found numerous problems," he says, including "expenses which appeared unreasonable."

October 22, 2001, in *Taxpayer dollars help fund many environmental groups*, Knudson reports—"Last year, about $137 million flowed to 20 major environmental nonprofit groups — an average of $377,000 a day — up 27 percent from 1999. Since 1998, more than $400 million in federal money has been granted to environmental groups." National Fish and Wildlife Foundation, Ducks Unlimited, The Nature Conservancy, and World Wildlife Fund received over two-thirds of that $400 million, and at least 15 nonprofits received a minimum of $1 million per year in federal funds.

While environmental groups that benefit from this government tax largess defend the practice as 'democracy', the fact that the lion's share goes to just four organizations spoils that argument. The possibility that these tax moneys may be involved with private land acquisition from less-than-willing sellers or cause unmitigated socioeconomic harm through changes in land use speaks sharply against calling this practice democratic.

The Nature Conservancy and Trust for Public Lands are just two of many private environmental organizations with the benefit of non-profit tax status, along with thousands of land trusts, that acquire rural land, help government acquire or control land, or cause land use to be changed. All these actions severely impact the sovereignty and well-being of land-based communities. This leads to the corporate and centralized government dependence that Means spoke about. It is painfully obvious that this threatens basic human rights and freedoms, while facilitating the globalization of natural resource industries.

Yet this *is* the strange fruit produced by an environmental industry that warns us about runaway industrial globalization, and monopolization of the food supply. The environmental industry, remember, is funded by big industry corporations, wealthy foundations, and government grants. So, this contradiction should not surprise people who have already experienced the deceitful, acquisitive habits of plutocrats in matters of land and financial opportunity. You can't always believe what people say, but you can always believe what they do. Let's look at a few environmental industry funders, and a few of their investments.

The Surdna Foundation, Inc., was established in 1917 by John E. Andrus with wealth from his gold, oil, timber, and real estate empire. Surdna's investment portfolio includes some 75,000 acres of Northern California timber production land. Andrus partners own an additional 90,000 acres of timber production land in the same area.

Yet Surnda contributed to Environment Now, a group that trains activist leaders to file appeals intended to block federal timber harvest. Surdna also made grants to groups that filed such appeals and stopped timber harvests and log supplies to mills in the Sierra Nevada area. Grants went to Sierra Club, Oregon Natural Resources Council, Wilderness Society, Western Ancient Forest Campaign, Audubon Society, and Natural Resources Defense Council.

What happened? In Northern California, 36 lumber mills shut down because of log shortages, causing unemployment for 8,000 people. Even though some of the harvest plans these groups appealed were in the same watershed as Surdna and Andrus partners' timber land, they did not file appeals on the plans submitted by Surdna. Timber values on Surdna land shot up. It reaped timber profits of $2.7 million in one year alone, a year in which other timber businesses were crushed. Surdna could then recycle these profits into more grants to environmental groups to wipe out even more of its small competitors.

Forest activist-journalist Jeffrey St. Clair and Alexander Cockburn investigated the stock portfolios of three top foundations that fund

environmental campaigns. Each of these foundations derived their
original wealth from multinational oil industries.

They found that Pew, with $3.8 billion in holdings, heavily invested
in timber, mining, arms, and chemical industries, in addition to oil
exploration. The Rockefeller Family Fund invested in at least 28
oil and gas development companies, and timber giants,
Weyerhaeuser and Boise Cascade. W. Alton Jones, they discovered, invested in a subsidiary of Maxxam - which was attempting,
at the time, to liquidate the largest single expanse of old growth
redwood remaining in private hands - and in Louisiana Pacific and
gold mining giant, FMC Corporation.

Other sources report that W. Alton Jones also invested in Atlantic
Richfield, Dow Chemical, Eastman Chemical, Eaton (aerospace
and defense), Ford Motor, General Motors, Georgia Gulf (chemi-
cals and methanol), IBP, Inc. (world's largest corporate beef and
pork producer), Kennametal (mining and highway equipment),
Lockheed Martin, McDonnell Douglas, Mead (controls 2.05 forest acres in the US), Mobil, Monsanto (agri-chemicals, patented
terminator seeds and patented genetically modified foods), Nor-
folk Southern (transportation, coal and timber), Phelps Dodge (gold,
silver and copper mining), Scotia Pacific (lumber), Union Pacific
Resources (oil and coal), USX-US Steel, Willamette Industries
(controls 1.8 million forest acres in the US), and YPF Sociedad
Anonima (petroleum and gas.)

St. Clair's and Cockburn's investigations uncovered a number of
situations where environmental compromises arranged by the
Clinton administration and environmental groups such as the Wilderness Society, directly benefited these foundations' holdings. This
is certainly 'high impact', strategic 'venture philanthropy'.

These examples provide a glimpse into the world of plutocratic
monopoly-building and cultural cleansing with the manifest destiny mindset—all in the name of Mother Earth. Indeed, they take
her name in vain.

*****

In *this* rural reality, family owned agriculture, small natural resource businesses and rural economies crumble piece by piece
with each new cost-prohibitive environmental regulation and job-
eliminating lawsuit that is funded by the fabulously wealthy. Each
time, rural communities protest that their socioeconomic needs
are not protected as required by the National Environmental Policy
Act (NEPA) or their state's equivalent policy.

However, the environmental industry and government agencies
alike dismiss these complaints with unrealistic socioeconomic analysis. They claim even remote rural communities can thrive on e-
commerce, eco-tourism and the retirement industry. This is all
tangled up with the federal land management agencies' fee dem-
onstration program that asserts it can replace moneys made on
natural resource harvest with charging the American public greater
and more widespread fees in order to enjoy their 'public' lands.

Despite the local jobs and businesses that will be harmed, the
required small business impact analysis are seldom realistic or
complete. The environmental industry and its partners in government thus claim they are helping, not harming. In reality, they
conquer without looking back, and move on to the next campaign.
Both the sovereignty and welfare of land-based communities are
thus discarded. A climate is created in which only massive corporations can afford to operate and even promotes the notion that
only those companies are environmentally friendly. With their small
competition collapsing, big business is merely enabled to grow
bigger.

Monopoly-builders have always funded campaigns for regulatory
pressure to eliminate their smaller competitors. But today this has
become a virtual formula for rural social and economic genocide.
Where old tensions might lay dormant or become evident between
Indian and non-Indian rural communities, the environmental industry takes advantage of these situations to prevent local alliances that might thwart the plutocratic outsiders' objectives. It is
a familiar old story.

When rural economies wither, joblessness at home forces rural
youth into urban assimilation. The community's socioeconomic

welfare declines as families continue to be stressed. Out migration toward urbanized population centers in search of family living wages proceeds until generational continuity is finally lost. If such a rural community is not well situated for high tourism traffic, it easily becomes a ghost town.

Programs offered to remedy this fatal socioeconomic hemorrhage prove insufficient. This is particularly true for rural communities within remote landscapes that the environmental industry targets for some special 'protected' status. As these communities continue to weaken in financial solvency and morale, they become ripe for acquisition by the rich and powerful. The American landscape is thus 'protected', cleansed of unwanted land dependent rural cultures.

*****

To the average urban American, the very idea of environmentalism eventually bringing about removal - or even any harm - of rural communities seems unbelievable. It certainly doesn't sound politically correct. After all, this is the 21st Century and our attitudes have progressed. Whether by force or finance, who today could possibly assume the right to make such highhanded judgments?

We would do well to remember that 'divide and conquer' tactics played a major role in the European conquest of the America's. Such is the nature of manifest destiny. Today the environmental industry also pits brother against brother. It divides rural people with contentious issues, entangling alliances and grant money. At the same time, it damages local non-tribal and tribal sovereignty, in both obvious and subtle ways.

The Environmental Grantmakers Association 1992 annual fall retreat Session 26 minutes reveal a truly heartless presentation and discussion of strategies to get rural natural resource producers and users fighting each other over access to natural resources. The privileged class believe it is their right to sow division among the 'common' people in order to achieve their own objectives. The minutes reflect some rather wild and contradictory speculation about how much money these working people that oppose them have at their disposal, and quite a bit of relishing just who might "hate" who that the EGA could take advantage of.

Speaking about the increasing grassroots resistance to the harm the environmental industry does to rural communities, Debra Callahan, then of W. Alton Jones Foundation, warns the EGA: "Then you come to the main stream message. And this is the one that really poses the threat to the progress of our community. And what that message says is man and nature can live together in productive harmony."

The message that man and nature can live in productive harmony threatens the EGA?!

Callahan goes on with her characterization of the people she and her EGA fellows put out of work. "And they were saying, and they were lookin' us straight in the eye, and they were saying, hey, because of the work that you've been engaged in, we're hurting, we're losing our jobs and it's not right. And how do you say to somebody, no, I don't want you to have your job? And when Joe Sixpack hears that message he goes, 'you're right, dammit, people oughta be able to work, and the environment ought to be able to be managed.'"

Joe Sixpack—this is apparently Ms. Callahan's term for working people. She speaks like a true elitist.

A few remarks by one Barbara Dudley insert a rare moment of confession to the EGA discussion. "This is a class issue. There is no question about it. It is true that the environmental movement is, has been, traditionally as someone said over the last three days sitting up at the podium, this has been in the past an upper class conservation, white movement. We have to face that fact. It's true. They're not wrong that we are rich and, you know, they are up against us."

Nevertheless, Callahan's advise to the audience for handling the broad-based working peoples' opposition to EGA oppression is "attack"—"find the ideological divisions" and "exploit them". She recommends smearing these folks by accusing them of right wing extremism. Callahan also talks about plans to get organized religion working against them, a familiar old manifest destiny strategy.

Callahan goes on to say, "We have to redefine the term federal lands to mean public lands. Federal is government, federal is bad. Public is all of us, it's a concept that we need to push. These lands that are at stake belong to all of us."

Indeed, the environmental industry media did just that. Doing so, however, is not just an opportunistic redefinition of federal lands, but a rather deceitful redefinition of *public* lands, too. Black's Law Dictionary, 5th Edition, defines public lands thus: "The general public domain; unappropriated lands; lands belonging to the United States and which are subject to sale or other disposal under general laws, and not reserved or held back for any special governmental or public purpose."

The overwhelming majority of federal lands 'redefined' by the environmental industry as "public" have already been appropriated and held back for a wide array of special governmental and public purposes, ranging from wilderness preservation to natural resource production. Thus they are not, according to law, public lands. Nor do they meet the legal definition's requirement of being for sale or other disposal. The plutocratic environmental elite intentionally "push" a misleading, false definition of the land on which small family livestock and wood businesses depend, so that the urban public feels compelled to chase these family breadwinners off the land.

Never mind that most urbanites don't even want to set foot on 'their public land'. EGA campaign dollars will determine how and what they think about that land. What the urbanites will think about it, given enough EGA dollars, is that those "Joe Sixpack" horse and cattle ranchers, sheepherders, loggers, firewood cutters, tree planters, miners, subsistence hunters, and mushroom, fern and berry pickers, had better get off the land. The elite's removal of workers from the land will be aided by finding their "divisions" and "exploiting them".

To defeat rural landowners' resistance against government regulation taking or reducing use of their land without fair payment for what is taken, Callahan advises the EGA to "find some wedge issues [to] at least neutralize them if not bring them over to our side." Once again, divide and conquer is her advice. This approach has applied to tribal property rights as well as non-Indian property rights.

All these divisive plans have been put into action in the years since. Even many church denominations have betrayed humanity and joined in the wilderness movement to remove rural people from the land. That should come as no surprise to the Indian nations. Such was and, obviously, still is the nature of manifest destiny.

The minutes of EGA's retreat Session 21, "Building an Environmental Majority", contain some very poignant comments from long-time Earth Day coordinator, Denis Hayes. His remarks show that the environmental industry leadership know exactly how they are harming land-based rural communities. Hayes told the assembled EGA participants—

"We need to more dramatically, overtly and profoundly incorporate into what we are up to, a sensitivity to the point of view of people. We have been more indifferent than we should have been about the pain that some of our policies have caused. If you drive through the Southwestern part of the state of Washington, you will pass hundreds and hundreds of little lean-to houses with crudely stenciled signs out in front of them that have painted across it, 'This Family Supported by Timber Dollars'. We've tended to view this as a fight against Plum Creek, a fight against Weyerhaeuser. And the people who have been thrown out of work have received less sensitivity from us than they should have."

Hayes appears blind to the big timber industry money that funds environmentalism, but at least he is not blind to the pain his chosen profession is causing the people who inhabit the rural landscape. He fully grasps that the environmental industry has really made war on and wrongfully characterized the little guy as the corporate fat cat. He continued—

"And in the Clean Air Act there was an effort proposed for political reasons, but I think, nonetheless, a good policy approach by Senator Robert Byrd to have what was in effect a Superfund for workers, the coal miners who would be thrown out of work by the provisions of that act. The environmental movement went along with that, and then double-crossed Byrd in the last two days of that fight, withdrew our support from the worker retraining provision, and the Clean Air Act went through without that."

Hayes obviously knows that the environmental industry betrays the little guy, his family, and his community, for its own apparent self-motivated political purposes. Their refusal to provide worker retraining is heartless and inexcusable. He goes on to recommend that this behavior cease, for both political and moral reasons—

"We can't continue to do that if we're going to have the kinds of sensitivities that allow to build a majoritarian movement— not necessarily because it's the majority of people who are affected by these things. A few timber workers here, in national terms, a few coal miners, but because the broad middle classes that we have to reach are sensitive to those kinds of issues. And most profoundly, because we as a movement have to do that because it's the right thing to do if we're to have a moral core to us."

To get the votes...and *if* they're to have a moral core... How did the EGA and company respond to Hayes' advice? Apparently, they *don't* have a moral core. Perhaps the crowd that was listening to Debra Callahan was so riled up with cries of 'divide!' and 'attack!' that they did not hear what Hayes was telling them. More likely, just like the infamous Marie Antoinette, they have no empathy and they just don't care.

Since their 1992 retreat, EGA and company kept right on harming rural communities. The only caring they demonstrate is the thinly disguised tactic that Callahan pushed, a tactic to divide natural resource providers and users against each other, using 'hooks' that pretend concern for their welfare. A number of EGA funded organizations for that purpose have sprung up in the years since.

As Callahan discussed, the EGA's own research shows that beseiged land-based communities were organizing in true grassroots fashion to defend the jobs, the land and the socioeconomic welfare that the environmental industry takes from them. Despite this knowledge, in 1994 the Environmental Working Group (EWG) widely distributed what was touted as their response to "anti-environmental myths". Here are just a few of the intentionally misleading claims—

EWG continues to broadcast that these people faced with loss of their jobs and lands are "really a loose coalition of industry lobbies and other special interests that create storefronts to make themselves look like grass-roots groups." That's *not* what Callahan said. And, since when do global industry lobbies have to be satisfied with loose coalitions? They've got Congress, the World Bank, the WTO and cheap foreign labor. They don't need rural America any more than the EGA does. As a matter of fact, they've got the EGA and the environmental industry, too.

EWG claims that government grazing fees "give an unfair competitive advantage to corporations and wealthy individual operators over small family ranchers, who must pay the full cost of grazing their cattle on private lands". Exactly the opposite is true. Enormously wealthy corporate livestock producers like EGA member Ted Turner have vast private land holdings. They don't need government land. But thousands of small Indian and non-Indian family ranch operations throughout the West will fold if their government grazing leases are terminated.

A very informative discussion of the difficulties facing Indian ranchers can be heard on the Internet by accessing the Native America Calling archives. Enter the web address http://www.nativeamericacalling.org/ and then click on land issues. When the listing of archived programs on land issues comes up, click on "The Plight of Native Ranchers", dated 1/13/00. If you ever doubted that 'Indian cowboys' love that life and want to preserve it, this program will set you straight.

Environmental Working Group insists that "the loss of thousands of jobs in forestry, mining, recreation, and other industries" are "fairy tales". Well, that's not what Callahan or Hayes said, either, is it?

Ironically, one of the few truths in EWG's piece is this: "In fact, environmental protection is a growth industry. Every year, the environmental industry grows by five to six percent and what is today a $200 billion a year international industry, is projected to rise to a $300 billion dollar a year industry by the end of the decade."

Got that? $200 billion for the global environmental industry in 1994, and $300 billion by 2000— growth industry and globalization in one. Obviously, it's a pay-off many are willing to lie for.

One more passage from Hayes' 1992 EGA presentation is particularly interesting: "People don't know where we want to go. And in fact, many of us don't have a very clear idea of where we want to go. We have been enormously effective at stopping things and constraining things, but we have not been very effective at coming up with an ideological context that expresses our values in terms of the science of ecology, with resilience and diversity and life as being dominant values that play themselves out throughout society's structures."

Hayes recognizes that the environmental industry has been very successful at stopping "things". Those things are called *rural livelihoods* - jobs - and the family and community security that those jobs provide. He recognizes that the industry has provided no inspiration for rural communities to accept this suffering. He goes on to speak of creating an inspiring vision—

"More importantly, we don't have a vision of the kind of society that we want to build. And we don't have any working models of how that society would function. And I think probably the most important thing that we need to give, is something that is non-threatening, something so that people can see an environmental, sustainable future that they really want to live in. It isn't mud floors and outhouses, but it's in fact a diversified, decentralized, resilient society."

Why Hayes would even think the rigid, centralized, big industry-enriched EGA would support creating a diversified, decentralized, resilient society, is somewhat of a mystery. It's obvious that society was actually far more diversified, decentralized and resilient before the EGA took over the environmental movement. Denis Hayes now, by the way, works for the fabulously wealthy Bullitt Foundation.

So what inspiring vision did the environmental industry then offer?— economic schemes like those presented time after time by people like Dr. Tom Powers. In this idyllic vision, rural land-based communities can easily give up the lands they depend on.

The land becomes government designated Wilderness Areas or National Monuments. Powers uniformly claims all these communities can replace their natural resource livelihoods with ecological tourism, computer-based home businesses, recruiting retired folks to move in, and developing cultural tourism.

The problem is, this cannot replace the entire economy of rural communities. Call it a pipe dream or call it a cruel sham. Either way, land-based rural communities are ultimately betrayed. The stresses this betrayal cause then magnify the conflicts resulting from government's overlapping promises of land, water and natural resources that comprise America's new war over land rights.

In the end, these ecological visions of rural utopia without 'dirty savage' natural resource users and providers perversely defies the entire reason land-based rural communities came to exist. It so resembles early colonialist visions of utopia without the 'dirty savage' that one can hardly fail to see it. If the environmental industry keeps going in this direction, someday its faithful followers will have to ask: Who grows the food, harvests the wood, mines the minerals and makes the things that feed, cloth, shelter and protect us?

What will the jaded environmental elite, secure in their stock portfolios, reply? 'This is the age of globalization. We have low-cost foreign labor to do those things. We don't need rural American communities or urban American labor. The rich can afford anything they want. The working poor have Walmart. The rest of you peasants have Salvation Army and Goodwill.'

When will WTO protesters, labor union members, human rights activists, small business owners, and, Indian and non-Indian land-based rural communities *all* see that we are struggling against the same people? When do we stop fighting each other over the crumbs that fall from the king's table? When do we tire of enriching the king, tire enough of it to unite? When do we stop believing in Marie Antoinette's mythical cake?

*****

What the urban majority don't know, and the environmental elite do not want them to know, is that the average inhabitant of the rural landscape is rarely the plunderer or over-consumer that so much environmental rhetoric focuses on. The people who inhabit the rural landscape on a multi-generational basis strongly value good stewardship of the land, the rural life, family and community, certainly far more than material gain and consumption. If not, they'd have abandoned the strenuous rural life.

Although rural people labor to provide for the faraway urban masses, there has always been a trend to under-compensate them, especially in agriculture. It is the guy further up the supply line, the chain of economic power, that gets rich. Ironically, it is these people who became the environmental grantmakers. It is bitterly ironic that rural people would be displaced to mitigate for the elite's abuse of the rural landscape, to simply be pushed aside by pluto-cratic monopoly-builders. Yet such is the nature of manifest destiny.

Generational rural communities, Indian or non-Indian, tend to have experience with financial hardship and the need to be frugal. They tend to recognize the need to preserve the land's bounty for future generations. A realistic ability to live self-reliantly on the land is vital to their communities' survival. In light of these commonali-ties, Winona LaDuke's presentation to EGA's 1992 Fall Retreat Session 21 should be thought-provoking.

LaDuke, from the White Earth Reservation, starts-out joking about wondering how dangerously to live with her remarks to the audience. Then she quickly points-out, "And I realize that about two-tenths of one percent of all foundation money goes to Indians. So I figured that I could live pretty dangerously because we haven't got that much to lose right now."

How curious. Two-tenths of one percent is a paltry sum for this astonishingly wealthy environmental industry that loudly proclaims its concern for Indian people—in the media. That's 0.2%. Sounds a lot like token beads and trinkets. Does the infamous deal for Manhatten Island ring a bell? Right here, we should realize that something is very much amiss in the environmental industry's attitude toward Indian people.

LaDuke tells the EGA about the people on her reservation: "...75 percent of our people hunt, 75 percent of our people trap or harvest from the land, we harvest wild rice, that's about 50 percent of our people....We're working the economy that we've had for thousands of years."

Unfortunately, Pew fellows like deep ecology-wilderness advocate, Reed Noss, who are chosen to provide the environmental industry's science, do not include humans in their vision of the wilderness landscape. Nor does much of the environmental industry approve of hunting and, especially, trapping. LaDuke, of course, is well aware of this. She talks about certain Indian people, people she considers environmentalists who fight for land, people the environmental industry does *not* consider environmentalists—

"...like an 82 year old Indian woman who lives in Nastasanin [Labrador]....she's standing on a runway, facing down a fighter jet that's coming towards her. This is a battle that went on for about 15 years where the Canadian government wanted to put a naval base on their land. And have low level flights. She's Inuit. She wouldn't be characterized as an environmentalist. But their struggle is very much about the land and the people living on the land, and keeping their ability to live there."

LaDuke knows the EGA would rather a naval base and low level flights occur on Indian land than *their* back yard. But this fight is

about the Inuit keeping a *realistic* ability to live on their land. She
goes on with a second example—

"...62-year-old Western Shoshone woman....Mary Dann. She
lives in a place called Newe Sogobia [Nevada], which is where
the Western Shoshone have lived for as long as they can
remember....The government wants to relocate the Shoshone and
take, essentially *steal* all their cattle, because the BLM says it's
their land, not Shoshone land....But their struggle - a community
that essentially is self-reliant, and if the government takes all their
cattle - it's about forcing a self-reliant community into welfarization,
in forcing them out of their own economy into the peripheries of
someone else's economy."

LaDuke knows that the environmental industry does *not* consider
cattle ranchers environmentalists and they fight family cattle ranching at every turn. Yet she says, "I suggest that both struggles are
environmental struggles." Thus she asserts that the ability to live
on the land in a self-reliant community is a genuine environmental
issue, and cattle ranching gives Western Shoshone that self-reli-
ance.

Her third example is a fight on the Blackfeet Reserve in Southern
Canada. "They'd been fighting for years a dam called the Old
Man Dam....on the Old Man River...the court ruled that they
required an environmental impact assessment on the dam. But
they did not require a halt in construction on the dam....And so
the Blackfeet....dismantled the old diversion of the river - that
had been taken *off* their reserve - brought most of the river back
into its original river bed, leaving the proposed dam site high and
dry."

Now there's a bold strategy. Diverting a river? Without an environmental impact statement, nonetheless? Now LaDuke's *really*
stretching the EGA's concept of environmentalism. So she says,
"It was a tactic about the Blackfeet *trying to just keep their
way of living*. But I suggest it would not be broadly construed in
the environmental movement, that Blackfeet would be considered
environmentalists. But I suggest that they are."

The fourth example LaDuke gives is that of Indians on many reservations fighting waste industry proposals to dump all manner of waste on their lands. She tells the EGA, "And a whole bunch of them have been defeated by people with no money, no resources, no offices and no phones, usually....Those people are not classified as environmentalists but I suggest that they are." Notice she points out these people got no money to help them do this. Apparently it's not an EGA priority.

Once again, LaDuke's example is about rural Indian land-based communities being realistically allowed to live self-reliantly on the land. The issue she is talking about here holds much in common with rural non-Indian land-based communities who also find themselves struggling to be realistically allowed to live self-reliantly on the land.

Indian reservations *are* tempting industry targets for all manner of toxic garbage and nuclear waste dumping. These battles are fought with nil help from the environmental industry. Perhaps it is simply a lack of caring. And maybe the lack of help is due to the not-in-my-back-yard syndrome. Nobody wants this stuff in their back yard. That's why huge barge loads of toxic garbage have been circling the globe for years.

Yet the environmental industry *is* quick to trot out their 'grave concerns' for Indians when it suits them. Fighting the Yucca Mountain nuclear storage proposal, which is key to Democrat success in elections, is a prime example. Yucca happens to be on land the 1863 Ruby Valley Treaty says *should* be the Western Shoshone's.

In fact, it looks like the reason Senator Reid (D-Nevada) canceled March 2002 hearings on his bill - which forces the Western Shoshone to give up their land claim - is because the Democrats suddenly needed Shoshone help to fight the Yucca proposal. Reid claims it's because he didn't know Western Shoshone were opposed to his bill, as though he'd never heard from them! But, it so happens that Senator Tom Daschle (D) had just found out he could not postpone the Yucca decision in Congress any longer, and he wasn't yet assured of enough legislators' votes to win. He needed clout - clout like the Western Shoshone's 1863 Ruby Valley Treaty.

Oops. Better let'em hang on to that treaty a minute....

This is not just my suspicious nature, folks. I ran this one by a
Western Shoshone tribal chairman, and *he* thought it was pretty
much on the bullseye. How likely were the Western Shoshone to
help Reid and Daschle out if they'd just had their land grabbed by
Reid, lost their grazing rights and their cattle, and were forced to
relocate?

And what happens after the Western Shoshone are no longer
needed by Reid, Daschle and company? Can you spell u-s-e-d?
Now that the Yucca Mountain nuclear waste facility is looking
like a done deal, Reid is back at shoving his bill down the Western
Shoshone's throats, and yet another dubious straw vote on the
controversial land payment that will extinguish the tribe's claim
has set the Western Shoshone homeland on its ear.

The tribe has gained support that surprises many unfamiliar with
Nevada rancher's issues. The Nevada Committee for Full Statehood and local non-Indian ranchers are supporting the tribe's land
claim and opposing BLM's confiscation of tribal members' cattle
and horses. What outsiders don't seem to fathom is that years of
lip service from the environmental community never did the tribe
a bit of good. Both the Western Shoshone grazers and the local
non-Indian grazers face the same oppression from federal land
management agencies. It is a natural alliance.

In the EGA session we're examining, LaDuke points out: "The
majority of atomic weapons that have been detonated have been
detonated on indigenous peoples." The people most subjected to
nuclear weapons testing happen to be the Western Shoshone. In
fact, I've read that where nuclear test bombs are concerned, they
are the most bombed people on earth.

The Western Shoshone's issue is one, obviously, of a rural land-
based community's realistic ability to continue living self-reliantly
on their land. It is an issue any rural community can relate to. Yet
such issues are not on the EGA's priority list. Perhaps that is
because the plutocratic EGA prefers promoting their wilderness
agenda over human rights.

LaDuke had remarked, "I think that the myth of America is *very* about that indigenous people do not exist." Most assuredly, in the environmental industry's wildlands vision they do not exist. Why fund big campaign coalitions to enable Indian communities to remain living self-reliantly on their land if you might rather see them replaced by wilderness uninhabited by humans? Such *is* the nature of plutocrats and manifest destiny.

LaDuke went on to speak about the attitude of "conquest", which is the manifest destiny attitude, really. "....I see that there is a rift that exists in this America. And it is something that continues to exist. It has to do with a concept of conquest. This is a society based on conquest. That underlies and permeates American values. The idea of the West, a frontier, a constant frontier— that is very much American. And it sets an adversarial relationship between the natives and the settlers."

The original conquest of the Indian nations itself, and government's conflicting promises of land, water, and resources - to both Indians and settlers - which followed, compounded with more recent promises of resources implicit in environmental law, set up some difficult-to-resolve adversarial situations. Yet they must be resolved in order for the local stakeholders - the Indian and non-Indian rural natural resource based communities - to survive.

Several forces can be seen taking advantage of these situations, to the detriment of the communities at stake. The environmental industry takes advantage of these situations to further pit natural resource-reliant groups against each other when it is to the industry's advantage. Conservative and liberal politicians alike, of course, make their fiery stump speeches; then move on to the next whistle stop and a different speech. Militant anti-government types may try to recruit desperate folks. And anti-Indian racists try to side with either the environmental industry or the non-Indian property rights community, whichever is to their advantage. Remember Debra Callahan's divide and conquer speech? The strategy's been around for thousands of years because it works.

LaDuke spoke about the concepts of conquest and constant fron-

tier that persist, causing adversarial relationships between Indian
and settler. Today's environmental industry, too, are offspring of
those settlers, inheriting those concepts. Their heavily financed
wilderness campaigns are trying to recreate the frontier. In
America's new war over land rights, they seek to permanently
create a constant wilderness frontier - in the name of Mother
Earth - by adversarial conquest of land-based communities that
rely on natural resource harvest to survive.

LaDuke goes on to talk about the underlying attitudes of conquest
and frontier that can still make people adversaries - enemies - of
land-based Indian communities today. "That relationship has existed for 500 years....what has happened is that people who live
in this American society have very much defined themselves historically, because it permeates American consciousness in an
adversarial relationship to the native. It is a historical relationship
and it exists today. I suggest that we have to challenge that. And
we have to undo that."

In view of the environmental industry's continued behavior in the
years since LaDuke's recommendations to the EGA, I suggest
that there may be more hope for changing this attitude in the general non-Indian public than changing it in the plutocratic EGA and
environmental elite. Non-Indian rural communities have much
more in common, more to motivate them, and more to gain by
resolving any conflicts they have with land-based Indian communities. The EGA-controlled environmental industry, on the other
hand, would have to voluntarily change its entire agenda dramatically, which plutocratic institutions just don't do, especially when it
would mean loss of revenue and control—hegemony. They certainly won't do it for self-sacrificing moral reasons.

LaDuke talks about moving on from the conquest-colonizer attitude to learning how to live on the land, responsibly and in community. She says that "somehow the settler has to quit being the
colonizer and has to figure out how to live here. I would suggest
that conquest is unsustainable, no matter what its underlying issues. The only thing that's sustainable is community. And that
existed thousands of years here and that's what we have to figure
out how to build."

What is appropriate to this transition from conquest - no matter what its underlying issues - to learning how to live on the land? Neither the underlying issues of plutocratic land abuse, which many EGA members' investments promote, nor plutocratic wilderness schemes, which EGA members fund and direct with their investment profits, have any appropriate place in this transition. They are both conquest-related, manifest destiny attitudes.

LaDuke asserts that community is really the only sustainable alternative to the conquest mentality, and that "we" have to figure out how to build it. The question I pose is, are "we" willing to do it? If "we" are the Indian and non-Indian land-based communities who are struggling to remain on the land, then I suggest that we do have much in common to motivate us.

If "we" is the EGA-controlled environmental community, it has shown absolutely no motivation to change its overall anti-human agenda for rural land. After all, they do not live and work on the land, they merely party on it occasionally. The rest of the time they hypocritically carry on in their urban castles as though they don't even use natural resources.

We should ask, has the EGA dramatically increased its funding for Indian issues since LaDuke's presentation to them in 1992? Have indigenous and Indian-defined issues become a major focus of powerful EGA-driven mainstream environmental industry campaign coalitions? Has the environmental industry given-up it's anti-Indian, anti-human wilderness campaigns, and stopped opposing Indian land acquisitions?

An examination of EGA member grants awarded and the evidence its major campaigns provide in the years since shows that very little has changed. Indigenous environmental justice advocates still receive token funding, token support, and frequently find themselves at odds with the environmental industry.

Peter Montague, writing for the Environmental Research Foundation in *Rachel's Environment & Health News #745, February 28, 2002, Headlines: White Privilege Divides the Movement,* brought us up to date on the EGA philanthropic foundations' giving to the broader field of environmental justice causes—

"The funding picture is indeed dismal....only $49 million (or 4%) goes to 'environmental justice' using the broad definition of the movement." This does *not* mean that indigenous issues receive even this insignificant 4%. Note that Montague says this is the giving to environmental justice causes *using the broad definition of the movement.* That means *any* organization that claims it is concerned with some aspect of environmental justice, *not* necessarily indigenous or Indian issues.

According to Luke Cole and Sheila Foster, in their book *From The Ground Up*, this loose definition would include "the movement encompassing civil rights and environmental racism; the anti-toxics (environmental health) movement; native American struggles for land, sovereignty and cultural survival; the labor movement for a safer workplace; a group of academics who began researching the disproportionate contamination of certain communities based on race and class...." and so on.

Essentially, then, foundation giving to *all* health, safety, minority and low income environmental justice issues is a mere 4%. As Montague points out, "The other 96% goes to the traditional legal/scientific environmental movement and the animal protection organizations."

He further explains, "In other words, the legal/scientific environmental groups are receiving substantial funding while the environmental justice movement is left to fight over what amounts to scraps that may fall from the philanthropic table." There you have it—the crumbs that fall from the king's table.

Evidently the EGA *still* values wilderness and animal rights *overwhelmingly* more than minority and low income humans. The disadvantaged are expected to fight over the scraps and bones the privileged toss their way. This can only mean that environmental leadership does not want to see environmental justice groups succeed. A decade after LaDuke's bold presentation to the EGA, the environmental industry is *still* the domain of the privileged class—hegemony.

This applies to both the 'radical' deep ecologist-animal rightist faction that oppose indigenous hunting and fishing rights, and the more 'mainstream' faction that oppose Indian land acquisitions and fail to support Indian environmental justice issues. Interestingly, both factions glorify the wilderness concept, support the anti-human wilderness movement and coalition to achieve its agenda. Their wilderness campaign has even expanded from land to now include glossy, high dollar "ocean wilderness" campaigns.

In fact, an indigenous organization called CERTAIN - Coalition to End Racial Targeting of American Indian Nations - now focuses attention on the human rights violations toward indigenous people these environmental organizations promote. CERTAIN was originally established in 1999 to counter "racially-based 'special rights' and 'termination' discourse targeting", which used to be the domain of the extreme right wing. But CERTAIN's website explains that it soon found things to be concerned about coming from environmentalism, as well—

"As time passed, research conducted independently of CERTAIN, and on CERTAIN's behalf, revealed that much of the underlying construction of arguments made by animal-rights groups, so-called 'deep ecologists' (or their other self-proclaimed title, 'biocentrists'), and other professedly anti-Native 'environmental' groups was rooted in the same elitist rhetoric that pervades the 'nature writing' of upper-middle- and upper-class Whites, primarily males, writing that emphasizes a false construct of an imagined 'pristine' wilderness positioned in direct tension with a similarly imagined construct of 'fallen' urban and industrial areas. In short, the imagined 'wilderness' is the refuge of the wealthy Whites who use it in respite from their work in the 'fallen' areas." Like I said, they don't live on the land, they just party here occasionally.

CERTAIN goes on to say that this "construct ignores the contested middle ground". I suggest that there is more potential and more to motivate non-Indian rural communities, who also now struggle to survive, to achieve that middle ground with indigenous communities. There is nothing to motivate the wealthy, plutocratic EGA-controlled environmental industry to consent to such a thing. After all, they do not live on the land, they just take from

it and vacation on it. Such is the nature of manifest destiny, plutocracy and cultural cleansing in the 21st Century rural landscape.

*****

Z Magazine published a piece about the Indigenous Environmental Network (IEN) by Zoltan Grossman in November 1995. It is
titled *Linking the Native Movement for Sovereignty and the
Environmental Movement.* The writer explains that the Network "is not simply a combination of the Native American movement with environmental activism" but that it has also "popular-
ized a new angle on Native sovereignty". Grossman describes
conflicts over such concepts as deep ecology, the role of humans
in wilderness, and subsistence hunting, that plague IEN's relationship with the dominant non-Indian environmental majority.

Deep ecology has a very disturbing anti-human undercurrent that
has been soundly criticized by social ecologist Murray Bookchin.
This anti-humanism finds subtle and open expression through opposition to indigenous hunting and fishing rights, and the anti-Indian slurs and threats that accompany such opposition. Deep
ecologists and wilderness activists are also philosophically opposed
to most modern uses of natural resources a tribe may pursue to
lift its membership from the poverty still imposed on so many.

Yet, donor records show that environmental justice groups depend on funding from the same EGA that finances the entire mainstream environmental industry and its wilderness and deep ecology ethos. However, EGA donor identity is sometimes obscured
from the group it chooses to fund by passing grant money through
an organization like the Tides Foundation to a larger environmental justice organization. The money is then rerouted to a local
Indian environmental activist group.

Tides president Drummond Pike told *Chronicle of Philanthropy*,
"Anonymity is very important to most of the people we work with."
Tides provides a selection of services that donors are told will
make their grantmaking "easier and more effective". Their web
site states, "Tides Donor Advised Funds provide an alternative to
direct giving or setting up a private foundation." Why is it to the

donor's advantage to avoid direct giving or setting up a foundation? Tides web site explains—

"Because Tides Foundation is a public charity, our Donor Advised Funds are exempt from certain limitations and penalties associated with private foundations, offering you the ability to play an active role in giving while enjoying substantial tax savings." In other words, Tides donors can have more *control* over how their donations are used than the law would allow through direct giving or a foundation—a typical plutocratic desire for hegemony.

Tides professes specific interest in "the struggles of indigenous people around the world who have pioneered ways of 'living gently' on the land." Yet the Institute for Deep Ecology Education was supported by Tide's services. Are we to believe that Tides is unaware of deep ecology doctrines that are so offensive to indigenous people?

This is the sort of thing that should arouse concern that the environmental industry may merely use Indian people to achieve its own elite environmental vision. The interest in indigenous peoples' ways of 'living gently on the land' can be seen in a flattering light. Or it can be seen as a threat in terms of how wilderness activists and deep ecologists tend to use this concept in support of their anti-human, uninhabited wilderness vision. However, Tides *appears* to support both ends of this spectrum.

Tides Center manages a number of environmental organizations as "projects", while Tides Foundation handles the money. Tides charges fees for its management services. Larger organizations receive grant moneys through Tides, then pass it on to smaller, local indigenous environmental justice groups.

Unfortunately, a potential problem with this kind of arrangement is that grassroots recipient groups could be quite disturbed if they learned that the identity of an anonymous donor was objectionable to them. They might even wish to refuse those funds on sheer principle.

How are recipients to know if their donor invests in activities they oppose, perhaps as much or more than they oppose the thing the donor has funded them to fight? How do they know if the donor invests in a company that competes with a company the group opposes? How do they know if the donor is just using their group to put its competition out of business? Well, if their donor's identity is hidden from them, they don't know these things.

Donors can use environmental groups to eliminate their business competition, as we have already seen. With donor identity hidden from view, this could easily take place without a recipient group's knowledge or consent. The potential for donors to abuse *unknowing* recipient groups like this is disturbing. It is also possible that a manipulative anonymous donor could actually pose unseen threats to tribal sovereignty and socioeconomic interests.

In the Z Magazine piece about Indigenous Environmental Network, Grossman says that the network groups "can more accurately be seen as the consolidation of grassroots traditionalist groups that have begun to build what eluded Native leaders such as Tecumseh and Red Cloud—intertribal unity against the most powerful forces running the United States".

Grossman's report refers to conflicts between some IEN network groups and their federally recognized tribal governments that have taken action or inaction the groups oppose. Sometimes the activists believe these governments are unfit, making charges that they are either non-traditional, illegitimate, desperate, corrupt, irresponsible, or even corporate fronts. Some believe they must refute their tribe's federally recognized government's right to govern, and that a different governing body not recognized by the federal government holds the legitimate claim to exercise tribal or political sovereignty.

Tribal sovereignty can be a difficult concept for some to understand. Grossman quotes IEN networker, Dine CARE, from its newsletter: "Sovereignty is a confusing issue, partly because politicians and bureaucrats have the wrong idea about sovereignty. There are two kinds of sovereignty. One is the so-called 'political sovereignty.' True sovereignty can only come from within...."

Obviously, there is more than one opinion of what Indian sovereignty means. Just as obviously, internal tribal sovereignty conflicts need to be resolved. However, it is certainly in any tribe's best interest that they be resolved internally.

These conflicts can present difficult obstacles to tribal unity on land, water and other natural resource issues. When such internal sovereignty conflicts exist and the conflicting sides voice their positions on natural resource issues to the public, it is no wonder that non-Indians can get confused about what Indian sovereignty means.

These conflicts and confusion about them can further complicate matters when governments' overlapping promises for natural resources cause conflict between Indian and non-Indian communities. When demands for land and water stemming from environmental laws or lawsuits are added to the mix, the conflicts and confusion are even further magnified.

The whole tangle of conflicts can, and sometimes does, tear rural America and its people apart. The social and economic damage that these complex conflicts can cause to Indian and non-Indian land-based communities, if left unresolved or allowed to intensify, should be a matter of great concern to both. It should be a human rights concern for both communities, and to human rights activists at large.

The plutocratic EGA-controlled environmental industry's private wealth and its influence on our centralized government's policy making solidifies the industry's position to fulfill its own envisioned manifest destiny and presumed higher purpose for the rural landscape. The industry's presumed higher purpose for the land leaves no room for the sovereignty needed by land-based communities to ensure their socioeconomic wellbeing.

*****

A broad view of the landscape brings into focus rural America's need to resolve its new war over land rights. It is still true that Indian America needs the unity that Tecumseh once sought. It is

also true that America's rural land-based communities as a whole
need that unity, too.

In reality, a policy of removal campaigns for alleged environmental purposes was established only a few decades after the Indian
Wars officially subsided. The ink had barely dried on western
Indian treaties when Theodore Roosevelt's conservation vision
soon led to forced removal of rural communities from the eastern
mountains to establish vast federally owned parks. Those were
not willing sellers being literally drug from their homes by law
enforcement officials and National Guard troops. Today, land-
based communities are subjected to enviro-economic warfare,
wilderness doctrine and land acquisition campaigns.

Indian and non-Indian alike, take heed. Such is the endless appe-
tite of manifest destiny.

Perhaps more today than ever before, local control or sovereignty
over decisions affecting the rural lands upon which we live and
labor is the most vital necessity land-based human communities
must secure in order to assure our socioeconomic welfare—our
very survival. That is a primary purpose of local sovereignty, and
it is the antithesis of manifest destiny. It is, in fact, a very basic
human right.

Plutocratic forces and manifest destiny mindset have run
roughshod over human rights for centuries in many guises. We
must counter this with an uncommon unity among the common
people of the landscape against which they are turned.

If not, our life on the land will fall to a second wave of manifest
destiny, a new cultural cleansing of people from the land. We will
be reduced to a state of neo-feudal tenancy in which only a handful may remain merely to serve and entertain the vacationing rich.
Even worse, for many, our life on the land will become a dream
completely lost in the great belly of urban assimilation.

Both have a historically familiar ring.

- Chapter Six -

Wilderness Doctrine

The roots of genocidal thought run deep throughout the history of human civilization. So too, the memories of peoples once subjected to genocide run deep, reminding society at large that elitist, genocidal thinking results in very real social horror.

Today, American society as a whole is sickened at events like the holocaust that ensued from Adolph Hitler's regime. Now we are on guard against the notion of Aryan supremacy. The American consciousness is growing in its recognition of the genocide perpetrated on the Indian nations. Nowadays, no sane member of our society would even think of defending slavery.

We have indeed made slow but sure progress in the field of human rights. Yet the roots of genocidal thought have not been eradicated, as they should, but still arise, sometimes to bear their bitter fruit in rather surprising places. Perhaps the most surprising haven of genocidal thought is within the very movement that once aspired to save the planet for humanity.

Murray Bookchin, director emeritus of the Institute for Social Ecology in Plainfield, Vermont, comments on this disturbing way of thinking within the movement. "The misanthropic strain that runs through the movement in the name of "biocentricity", antihumanism, Gaian consciousness, and neo-Malthusianism threatens to make ecology, in the broad sense of the term, the best candidate we have for a 'dismal science'." We can turn to a conservation biology textbook to see how dismal this science has become.

That this anti-human attitude within the movement is not just a phenomenon limited to a few radicals, but is even held by biocentric professionals, is illustrated in the words of Malcom L. Hunter, Jr. Hunter comments on this mindset on page 355 of his conservation biology textbook, *Fundamentals of Conservation Biology*. "Conservation biologists are constantly reminded of what our species has done to extirpate or threaten other life-forms. This awareness seems to make some conservation biologists a bit misanthropic. Or perhaps it is the other way around; maybe people who are not particularly fond of humanity are more likely to select careers in which they interact with other species."

Just how far afield from human rights thinking this lack of fondness for humanity can lead is revealed in Hunter's epilogue on page 411. "If you can fully embrace a biocentric perspective, you can be heartened by the fact that the harm our species has brought to other organisms is largely insignificant in the long term. A few hundred million years from now a visitor to planet earth will probably be barely able to detect that *Homo sapiens* ever existed. For some people, it may be comforting to have this big picture in view because it offers a path to freedom from despair over the state of life on earth."

In this mindset, any notion of despair for the plight of humanity is so eclipsed by despair for the earth that humanity's continued existence itself becomes the earth savior's ideological enemy. Here, Hunter alludes to the thinking that manifests at its most radical perimeters, not just by various and sundry acts of sabotage against targeted businesses, but by the too-bizarre shock-talk of the so-called Voluntary Human Extinction Movement.

For fervent adherents to the most dismal biocentric perspective, whether professional biologist or eco-anarchist, the thought of humanity's disappearance is "comforting". After an examination of the entire modern environmental milieu and its leadership, one indeed wonders who among them will truly defend humanity.

Dr. Reed Noss, a co-founder of the Wildlands Project, writes on page 18 of *A Citizen's Guide to Ecosystem Management*: "Humans are indeed part of the ecosystem, but modern humans – or perhaps any humans in large numbers – are more like a cancerous tumor than a healthy organ..."

Conservation educator David Orr says, "It is humans that need to be managed, not the planet." And what sort of management is recommended by modern leaders of conservation science? Noss writes for the Wildlands Project, in *Land Conservation Strategy*, "I suggest that at least half of the land area of the 48 coterminous states should be encompassed in core reserves and inner corridor zones (essentially extensions of core reserves) within the next few decades." He says this is a "reasonable guess" of what it will take to restore ecosystem health "assuming that most of the other 50 percent is managed intelligently as buffer zone."

As if this goal is not alarming enough in terms of potential human rights violations, Noss goes on to call for even more. "I would offer a more ambitious long-term goal, pending human population reduction, that at least 95 percent of a region be managed as wilderness and surrounding multiple-use wildlands." The term "multiple-use wildlands" is a rather misleading, disingenuous term. Wilderness doctrine allows virtually no human use of the land but backpacking, cross-country skiing and snowshoe trekking reserved for those physically and financially able to access the land totally on foot.

Human rights advocates should also pay attention to the biocentrist's notion of "human population reduction". The many ways in which this "human population reduction" might occur require a watchful eye. In his textbook, Hunter quotes from Shakespeare's *Merchant of Venice* in support of the biocentrist's argument. Yet the bard's words - "You take my life when you take the means whereby I live" - are far more relevant both in context and poignancy to the human inhabitants of the rural landscape. You take their lives when you take a land-based people's means to make a living on the land.

Their lives are incrementally taken by increasingly punitive and cost-prohibitive regulation that pushes them off the land in favor of the ultra-rich. Or they may be taken more suddenly by raging infernos roiling across the landscape, wildfires brought on by a decade of pervasive no-timber-cut, anti-grazing bias. Not only will there be no timber jobs on millions upon millions of incinerated forests and grasslands that are intentionally allowed to build up fuels until disaster strikes, but there will be no livestock grazing either. The lives of rural peoples are being taken once again in this age of enviro-economic globalization.

Ironically, the land itself is stripped by the very campaigns, lawsuits and policies of those who claim to be saving the earth from rural humans. Soils are sterilized in the stupendous heat of catastrophic wildfire. The watersheds are destroyed and the wildlife is burned to a crisp, virtually by the whim of the same people who squeeze rural families off the land with endangered species lawsuits.

This is not how the urban majority are told the environmental industry is affecting the earth or rural communities. Yet it is the reality manifesting in the rural landscape. Land-based communities need to gain a greater voice and represent their concerns in greater numbers.

Wilderness doctrine will continue to demand increasing expansion of wilderness, excluding more and more people from their lives on the land.

Wild Earth magazine is the publishing mouthpiece for the Wildlands Project. Dr. Micheal Soule writes that the publication's role in the Wildlands Project is "to constantly remind the various wilderness groups that the core-buffer-wilderness proposals they are developing are merely emergency plans".

He says, "Wild Earth writers and editors will constantly challenge proponents to design and implement ever more expansive reserve plans."

Dave Foreman, another co-founder, explains the Project's goal. "The role of individuals and grassroots groups is to develop proposals for Wilderness Recovery Networks on the regional and ecosystem level using the Noss model so that such plans can dovetail into similar plans for adjacent regions until the continent-wide plan is assembled." Every political, court-related and PR strategy is then used to implement the cooperator groups' vision for the land.

This vision, however, is not the vision of the land's generational inhabitants, but largely the vision of strangers to the communities its fulfillment will erase. One feature of that vision is road-ripping, the elimination of roads from areas targeted for some form of wilderness designation. The Kettle Mountain Range here in remote Ferry County, Washington, has been a continual wilderness target.

Now all of rural Washington is reeling at the cost of the state's controversial new "Forests and Fish" rule, originally initiated by federal agencies, that requires an $80,000 per mile upgrade on private roads that don't comply with new standards. The option for those who cannot afford the upgrade is to "abandon" the road according to specifications. It requires that roads abandoned not simply be blocked off, but must be 'restored to natural conditions', also at a high cost. Fines, imprisonment and/or loss of their land will result for those who cannot afford to comply.

The rule is worthy of the road-ripper's vision— it will reduce the human population in the rural landscape. That the vision threatens to squeeze the most financially vulnerable off the land first, and less than graciously, apparently matters little.

Foreman wrote for the Wildlands Project, "Nature Conservancy staff should be plugged in so that gaps in reserve networks can become priorities for acquisition." Noss wrote that in many cases private land would "need to be acquired and added to national forests and other public lands". He elaborated that wilderness groups' proposals should "indicate actions that must be taken in order to secure the system".

The actions specified include land and mineral rights acquisitions, wilderness or other reserve designations, road closures, and cancellation of both grazing leases and timber sales. This is why we see the environmental grantmakers pumping billions into anti-mining, anti-logging, anti-farming and anti-grazing lawsuits and cam-

paigns. It removes the little guy, the non-elite, from the rural landscape.

The industrial elite, however, continue to expand and prosper, both
here and abroad. Neither the elite nor the common citizen cease
to consume mined, farmed or logged products. They merely buy
from the surviving big industry winners, or export their environmental responsibility and our natural resource and manufacturing
livelihoods to the developing countries least likely to protect the
environment and most likely to abuse their labor force.

As a people, we must regain a sane perspective on domestic natural
resource issues. We cannot safely continue to act as though we
do not need or use natural resource products. This hypocritical,
NIMBY ecological outlook is harming our land-based rural communities, causing harmful dissension, and harming the entire
nation's domestic food and natural resource supply security. It
benefits only the super-rich.

Human rights proponents should look closely at these actions that
are heavily funded, year after year, by a privileged elite with hefty
investment portfolios. How many stand to profit from the misfor-
tune of small rural natural resource provider communities? How
have the promises to remote rural communities that eco-tourism
and e-commerce would replace their traditional livelihoods panned
out? Hideously. What is this likely to mean for Indian Country
and all of rural America as we head down this road?

Years ago, Noss said, "Conservation biology and landscape ecology are both young sciences and show many signs of immaturity,
such as theoretical confusion." These theories and their adherents' theoretical confusion are proving harmful to land-based communities' socioeconomic welfare. The adherent's twisted rural
economics rhetoric is really just another chapter in genocidal
doublespeak. It does not provide a realistic life on the land.

Every socio-political change movement has its mainstream proponents that serve to gradually assert change on the populace,
along with its extremist propaganda that serves to continually push
the envelope. In biocentrist politics, the extremist viewpoint is

represented by pronouncements that are so anti-human it is tempting to dismiss them, to deny any possibility that they may influence our lives. Yet just as Aryan supremacy rhetoric should not be dismissed as harmless, neither should the anti-human rhetoric of extreme biocentrism be ignored.

As the public is desensitized to the rhetoric of old extremist groups, new and more extreme entities arise to ratchet-up the propaganda. We have seen Earth First! and PETA's once-shocking actions and rhetoric eclipsed by those of the Earth Liberation Front (ELF) and the Animal Liberation Front (ALF).

Today the rhetoric of the Voluntary Human Extinction Movement (VHMNT), Gaia Liberation Front (GLF) and Church of Euthanasia ratchet-up the anti-human sentiment even further. "As VHMNT volunteers know, the hopeful alternative to the extinction of millions, possibly billions, of species of plants and animals is the voluntary extinction of one species: Homo Sapiens…us." VHMNT spokesman's twisted rationalization: "Extinction of the human race on earth doesn't mean an end to humanity. Extinction is in accordance with God's plan for us."

This is certainly a perverse theology. It's motto is, "May we live long and die out." But some are in a hurry for humanity to die out.

Gaia Liberation Front says it advocates human extinction by "hand-to-hand combat, or better yet, biological agents that kill only humans". Church of Euthanasia recommends humanity extinguish itself with suicide, abortion, cannibalism and sodomy. Its one "commandment" is "Thou shalt not procreate." It sounds too extreme to take seriously, but reading VHMNT's deep ecology website is like reading a brainwashing program. There are certainly people vulnerable to this kind of rhetoric.

Each new generation's "rebels" require a cause more shocking than the preceding generation, particularly those children of privilege who have no real socioeconomic suffering of their own. For some, championing some other oppressed segment of humanity is no longer enough. Gaia Liberation Front speaks as though it has searched in vain for some small segment of humanity worthy of preservation, but even "primitive" societies offend because they may sprout a technological bad seed:

"Shouldn't we make exceptions for tribal peoples, who are living in harmony with nature?....No, because they're all Humans. Remember that those basic technologies were invented independently by Humans of different races, in the new world as well as in the old. And remember that the Humans, Europeans included, were all tribal once."

The proponents of extreme biocentrism and wilderness doctrine have pondered themselves into a paradox wherein the human species as a natural species should be saved, and yet it is their ideological enemy. So some believe that humanity is the only natural species that should be considered for extinction. Some are so unable to envision humanity capable to thrive in harmony with the earth that they raise the scientifically and spiritually radical theory that humanity is an alien species.

GLF says, "The Humans technological propensities are probably genetic, because their basic technologies....have all appeared independently more than once. The Humans come into full view, then, as a *hostile* alien species, *programmed* to kill the planet." GLF concludes, "While we support all voluntary efforts to make the humans extinct, we do not exclude the involuntary route."

Is this harmless ranting or a dangerous genocidal influence?

Well, Wild Earth magazine is the publishing mouthpiece for the Voluntary Human Extinction Movement as well as the Wildlands Project. Columbiana magazine, published in Washington state's Okanogan highlands and posted on the web, "is proud to provide links with....the Voluntary Human Extinction Movement" right along with more mainstream entities like Kettle Range Conservation Group, The Lands Council, Okanogan Highlands Alliance, Northwest Ecosystem Alliance, Washington Wilderness Coalition and many other groups active in biocentrist-inspired campaigns and lawsuits.

Wild Earth's spring 2000 issue listed a raft of mainstream environmental organizations cooperating to plan the Rainforest to Rockies (R2R) portion of the Wildlands Project: American Lands Alliance, Coast Range Association, Gifford Pinchot Task Force, Hells Canyon Preservation Council, Northwest Ecosystem Alliance, Oregon Natural Resources Council, Washington Trails Association, Central Cascades Alliance, Friends of the Gorge, Grant County Conservationists, Kettle Range Conservation Group, Oregon Natural Desert Association, Siskiyou Regional Education Project, and the Wildlands Project itself.

This does not look like an insignificant influence.

The wilderness movement continually chants its "pre-European conditions" mantra for the environment. It appears to be one more race-tinged sound bite intended to divide the inhabitants of the rural landscape against each other to prevent their common defense. While all wilderness proponents may not advocate extinction of humanity, they do all intend to manage the human population according to their wilderness vision.

Roger G. Kennedy suggested at the National Wilderness Conference in 1994 that religious people should be cultivated as allies to the wilderness movement. James Nash, a Methodist environmental minister in Washington, DC, says, "The church should be the prime model of ecological ministries to the world." Thus "wildlands theology" is now literally preached as one's religious duty across Christendom.

The list of religious figures and organizations now advocating the removal of rural timber workers and family ranchers from federal lands is staggering, sobering.

Christendom's embrace of the wilderness movement and its twisted anti-human wilderness theology is the icing on the genocidal cake. Just as the original conquest of Indian America was justified with religious rhetoric, so the second wave of Manifest Destiny is justified by its new wilderness doctrine.

It has a familiar ring....too familiar for any sincere Indian treaty rights or human rights advocate to ignore.

Wilderness doctrine is the same old genocidal manifest destiny doctrine dressed up in flowery biocentric jargon. These people are no loyal allies of land-based peoples. Beware of this same old deceptive voice of genocide. It's just another Custer in green gear.

Chapter Seven

Sovereignty and Environmental Justice

It is obviously important that tribal governments make informed and judicious natural resource use decisions. It is also vitally important that tribal sovereignty, without outside interference, be fully upheld with regard to tribal decisions on reservation lands. Only this can fulfill tribal governments' obligation to the overall socio-economic welfare of tribal members. Tribal government must see to it that tribal members are enabled to realistically live and work upon their tribal lands.

While the historical understanding that Indian tribes are sovereign nations is correct, this understanding sometimes obscures, especially from non-Indians, certain demographic realities of tribal governance. Where land use decisions are concerned, particularly in terms of land area and directly affected population, tribal sovereignty represents self-determinate governance at the local or landscape level. In this particular aspect, tribal sovereignty also is similar to the original purpose of local or county governance.

In other words, the elected government representing those living and working on the land in question, those most directly affected, must be empowered to make local land use decisions in order for the local population to retain their basic human right to control their own socioeconomic welfare. Anytime the people living and working on the lands affected by a land use decision are divested of this right, or this right is somehow interfered with, gross violations of human and civil rights are bound to occur.

119

This sovereignty principle, which is central to the socioeconomic welfare and very survival of tribal peoples, is often prominently stressed by a plethora of mainstream environmental and environmental justice organizations when commenting on land use decisions throughout Indian country. In view of the extensive activism practiced by many of these organizations, intended to influence land use or natural resource decisions far from the lands on which the activists themselves reside, the question of whether or not these organizations always practice respect for tribal sovereignty bears close examination.

BIA reformer Kevin Gover, along with Jana Walker wrote: "This is what we find troubling in the 'environmental racism' issue. Too often, the environmental community appoints itself the officious protector of the Indians....To people like ourselves, Indians who have devoted our careers to the defense of Indian rights, this is unspeakably arrogant."

The point at which the involvement of such organizations might depart from supporting tribal sovereignty to constituting interference with tribal sovereignty requires both general and case-by-case investigation.

Indigenous environmental justice activists often quite appropriately criticize non-Indian environmental organizations for practicing environmental elitism, accusing them of unwillingness to relinquish a privileged status as controllers of natural resources which rightfully belong to tribal peoples. Environmental opposition to the traditional Makah whale hunt, and Sierra Club's opposition to the White Earth Land Recovery Project are glaring cases in point. The environmental mainstream's heavily funded wilderness movement itself is broadly denounced by indigenous environmental activists as an anti-sovereignty, anti-indigenous campaign riddled with Indian and human rights violations.

When examining controversies that arise around tribal natural resource use proposals or decisions, whether or not the activism of even indigenous environmental justice organizations may be interfering with, rather than supporting, the tribal sovereignty process, must also be carefully examined. It is important to examine what influences may motivate all the organizations and elements involved, in general and in specific circumstances, in order to determine whether these are welcome influences within the tribal decision making process.

Maintaining the principle of tribal sovereignty requires that each tribe's sovereignty must be protected from all outside interference, even from members of other Indian tribes if necessary. At what point might outside environmental justice organizations become guilty of practicing elitism, a desire to control other tribes' lands, an elitism for which they have criticized both non-Indian environmental organizations and various business interests? At what point might such an organization's portrayal of tribal councils, whose decisions they oppose, as victims of environmental racism or scandalously corrupt, depart from truth to subversion of the sovereignty process?

Further, at what point might even a local environmental justice group become guilty of interference with their own tribe's sovereignty process by enlisting outside influence to pressure or even force tribal decisions to conform with a minority opinion of what is best for the tribe? Again, it is vital that influences on these local groups be examined by tribal members and tribal government in order to determine if they are welcome influences which enhance tribal sovereignty and self-determination.

These situations need to be examined carefully on a case-by-case basis in order to assure that tribal sovereignty and self-determination is truly upheld. Outsiders should respect the tribal sovereignty principle, and tribal members should strive to resolve such conflicts within the tribal governance process in order to protect the sovereignty principle.

An examination of all the environmental organizations and other businesses or organizations involved in a particular controversy, an exploration of how and why they became involved, and a thorough look at their financial sources and political agendas is necessary in each different situation. One situation may prove to be a case of government or military-industrial elitism exerting unwholesome influence, while another may prove to be a case of environmental elitism seeking to abuse tribal peoples and subvert their right to self-determination.

A very close examination of the actual tribal membership's stance, rather than the opinions of outsiders, and the tribal government's rationale, should also be instructive. Controversies of this nature must be viewed within the context of tribal sovereignty *and* tribal government's obligation to safeguard the tribe's socioeconomic welfare in the best manner possible.

The Bush administration's recent proposal to tap oil deposits beneath the Arctic National Wildlife Refuge (ANWR) brought all of these various types of organizations into play. Here we have a situation in which one indigenous group, the Inupiat, favor oil exploration in their portion of the ANWR, and a second indigenous group, the Gwichin, who are opposed to the Inupiat's drilling proposal. Even more confusing to onlookers is that the Gwichin themselves propose oil exploration on their own lands in another location.

As the larger political battle over ANWR drilling raged on, both groups were used as examples of why or why not Congress should approve oil exploration in the ANWR. Now that Congress has rejected the broader proposal to drill in the ANWR, the Inupiat will press on with their oil extraction goal. Thus the conflict will be between the two indigenous groups, and the various interests who ally themselves with each.

This presents particular challenges to preserving the overall sturdiness of indigenous rights of self-determination and sovereignty. While the controversy will likely be played out in the public eye, enlisting outside help to influence the final decision, it would be much better for the future safety of indigenous sovereignty if the two indigenous groups were to resolve the matter between them without undue outside influence. Seeking outside advice, rationally, is not the same thing as seeking to bring outside pressure to bear on internal matters of indigenous sovereignty and self-determination. By the same token, outsider's merely expressing an opinion must be differentiated from outsider's seeking to pressure or force a certain tribal decision.

It seems to me there is a fine yet obvious line in such matters if respecting and promoting the sovereignty principle and that of self-determination is one's concern. I am reminded of Mean's statement that you can't really talk about environmental responsibility until you secure freedom. Freedom, self-determination, sovereignty, are what empowers, enables and necessitates responsible decisions with respect to the environment and all other matters pertaining to the socioeconomic welfare of land-based peoples.

In terms of freedom engendering environmental responsibility, that means owning the power to exercise local control by both traditional wisdom and developing a successful body of place-specific management science. Only by having such power can land-based communities protect both the natural environment and their communities best overall interests. Relying on outside science is fraught with pitfalls.

A few years ago the Atlantic Monthly published an expose of corporate funding, influence and control of not just the expected industrial science, but even university science and research. In chapter five I discussed EGA corporate and foundation funding and influence of environmental science. That these powerful influences exert any control whatsoever on science that somehow becomes law and exerts power over the less privileged inhabitants of the land should concern the public.

Also broadly known and acknowledged are the inherent dangers of blanket management policies, no matter how well intended they may be. Environmentalism has worked itself into a theoretical conundrum. It started out saying that every minuscule ecosystem is inherently unique and preservation-worthy in its complexity of inhabitants and interactions, and ended up saying that in order to protect all this inherently vital biological complexity we must enforce universal standards.

However, the leadership of land-based communities must provide for the realistic ability of its members to live on the land. It cannot rely on politicized theoretical science. Community leadership must somehow assure that both the uniqueness of the land base is protected while assuring that the people can realistically live there. If they are prevented from achieving this, the people suffer and so will the land. The two are intertwined.

Preventing the land-based community from experiencing the harm that is caused by influences at cross-purposes with local socio-economic welfare is a basic necessity which can only be assured by local control of place-specific science and management practices. Blanket policies and dogmatic adherence to theory rather than reproducible fact are dangerous ruts to be avoided. The bottom line is that proven science is the only science land-based communities can both afford *and* survive.

There are probably no environmental issues more controversial or emotional than those involving nuclear materials or military-industrial toxic wastes. These are issues that concern me as a person whose homeland contains the universally infamous Three Mile Island nuclear facility in the midst of the Susquehanna River, now living not quite that close to the also infamous Hanford nuclear facility. So, it is not hard for me to understand the temptation to bring in outside help in toxics cases if tribal leadership seems to be heading in an unwise direction. Yet it is still terribly important to do all that can be done to resolve such disputes internally in order to preserve the overarching sovereignty necessary to the tribe's continued survival and future socioeconomic welfare.

The subject of toxics cleanup on Indian land does not appear to be a very high priority of the wealthy corporations and foundations who fund the environmental industry, the environmental industry itself, or the federal government. On the greater stage of environmentalism, the indigenous environmental justice activists appear to stand alone in this issue. Superfund-type cleanup is proceeding at a snail's pace across America. This is likely one issue that tribal governments, tribal members, non-Indian neighbor communities and the general public can all agree upon.

This is one area of environmental responsibility that the affected communities must apparently empower themselves to address with little help from the distant privileged economic class. That this is so lends proof to Means' assertion that we cannot really talk about environmental responsibility until we secure freedom.

So all questions of environmental responsibility must be examined through the eyes of self-determination and the sovereignty principle. This is government directly from the landscape up rather than from the top down, and precisely the opposite of plutocracy, as well.

Part Three

The New War Over Land and Water

Think on this, brothers. Put aside our anger. Put aside your fear. Put aside your vain hopes.

Think without prejudice of what I have said here and it will become clear to you as it is to me why the very leaves of the forest drop tears of pity on us as we walk beneath.

And after you think on it, remember this: any child can snap with ease the single hair from the horse's tail, but not the strongest man, nor the wildest stallion, can break the rope woven of those same hairs.

Tecumseh, Shawnee

- Chapter Eight -

Fish Versus Tribes

Could today's "fish versus farmers" environmental lawsuits become tomorrow's "fish versus tribes" lawsuits? You may think it's unlikely, but it could happen if some staunch wild salmon activists deem it necessary. Use of a Public Trust Doctrine lawsuit has been stoutly recommended to further anti-hatchery wild salmon activist goals. One must wonder whether the doctrine might be combined with domestic environmental law or international environmental agreements to supersede Indian treaty rights in the courts. That is a question yet to be answered.

However, there is discernible activity on several fronts that could result in a case before the courts to set just such a precedent. Such a ruling would essentially say property rights reserved by Indian treaties for land, water or some other natural resource (such as food sources like fish, whale, deer, elk and so on) are superseded by domestic environmental law, international agreements or other such laws, as matter of public interest, or public trust.

Some believe the chances are remote, and some clearly do not. Yet, lawmaking and interpretation have a way of surprising us. If such a precedent is set, a Pandora's box will be stuck open for all rural land, water and natural resource owners. Indian and non-Indian land-based communities alike, will lose socioeconomic well-being and self-determination.

Originally a legal triumph for the average public, Public Trust Doctrine goes back far beyond the birth of the US to English common law, which gave the public rights to navigate and use waterways for purposes like fishing and hunting. Such "submerged lands" were held by the Sovereign subject to public rights. In the US, such submerged lands were passed to the state upon statehood, subject to the same limitations for the benefit of the public. In its early days in the US, the doctrine was initially applied to large areas of water like ports and bays.

Today's new set of promises for land, water and natural resources for the environment are based on government's power to make laws intended to safeguard the public's best interest. Particularly where water bodies are involved, many believe that environmental law is backed by public trust doctrine.

In recent years, the doctrine has been interpreted to apply to an increasing variety of public purposes, including water resources, or instream flow, for fish. In the famous Mono Lake case - National Audubon Society v. Superior Court of Alpine County (1983) - Los Angeles was required to reduce its water withdrawals from Mono Lake tributaries so the lake's fish habitat could be restored.

On the Washington State University web system, an education page on "Public Trust Doctrine", makes the following statements (italics emphasis added):

"The Public Trust Doctrine may very well become *the most important tool* for citizens seeking to protect their streams and rivers….Public Trust Doctrine defines the state's responsibility to protect the 'navigable waters' and lands that are held in the public trust. In some states, *even tributaries* of 'navigable waters' are included."

"Environmentalists can use the Public Trust Doctrine to challenge state decisions and actions….*Probably the most potent feature of the Public Trust Doctrine is that it can override prior water rights….*"

"The Public Trust Doctrine can also be *used as leverage* during policy deliberations and public scoping sessions and hearings….If the agencies fail to provide a more environmentally benign alternative, then you can bring up a *Public Trust lawsuit.* Although the court process may be long and arduous, *many important precedents have been established."*

"The Public Trust Doctrine may very well emerge as *the most comprehensive* river protecting tool available to the river activist. *Its strength is evident in the fact that it can override senior water rights in the name of the public trust."*

We have a history, in this country, of issues that are framed as greater public interest issues being used to overwhelm and violate individual and tribal prior rights. Theodore Roosevelt essentially said it long ago, in his autobiography, when he inferred that Indian issues interfered with his duty as 'steward of the whole people'. Since Teddy and fabulously wealthy names like Rockefeller kicked off the initial federal environmental movement, we should take note of its roots in taking land and water from the less privileged rural populace in the name of the "whole people".

Here we find the familiar old roots of an outlook that rationalizes removal and usually disbursed relocation of entire rural land-based communities in the name of the greater public good. In application, it was and is nothing less than cultural genocide.

If an environmentally-based public trust lawsuit defeats treaty rights, Indians as property owners - owners of prior reserved rights to land, water, hunting, fishing and gathering - will lose because such a precedent would expose all their treaty rights to the possibility of the same defeat. Non-Indian land and water owners will lose because the very constitutional foundation of their property rights will be fatally wounded.

The same US Constitution that protects non-Indian property rights recognizes the federal government's power to make international treaties, treaties with other sovereign nations. This is what the Indian treaties were and still are—international treaties between the US and various sovereign Indian nations. Thus the property rights guaranteed in Indian treaties are protected by treaty and the Constitution.

As a result of Winters vs. United States (1908), Reserved Rights Doctrine, or prior reservation doctrine, also protects Indian tribes' various rights to water. Non-Indian water rights are protected in various states either by Riparian Doctrine, Doctrine of Prior Appropriation, or a combination of both known as the California Doctrine. Treaty property rights to water are considered most senior of these water rights because their founding date has been established as "since time immemorial".

As such, *if these treaty water rights, or any other such natural resource treaty rights, can be defeated* by environmental laws or international agreements with the force of public trust doctrine, *non-Indian natural resource owners, lacking the added legal clout of an international treaty, cannot expect their rights to survive in the future.* Solidly framed as a public trust interest, the combined powers of environmental law, international environmental agreements, eminent domain and government condemnation could then be directed against any and all rural land-based communities with no further legal impediments.

So the fact that the environmental industry has made substantial gains in framing their demands for natural resources as a public trust issue in the media the public sees every day, and in the courts, should raise concern. Today, we claim to be in an era of increased sensitivity to human rights. Yet it contradicts the most basic notion of public interest and public trust that the actual lobbying, lawmaking and precedent-setting court cases that establish these promises for environmental purposes, are funded and directed with the wealth of the same privileged elite that have a tight leash on environmental organizations, the business economy and politics.

This is essentially the same class that funded and directed the initial conquest of the Indian nations, justified by the manifest destiny rationale, and the subsequent conquest of small business and rural land-based communities, perhaps best described as enviroeconomic globalization. It is not surprising, therefore, that manifest destiny rhetoric was essentially merged with public interest rhetoric after the initial conquest of Indian America was accomplished.

Manifest destiny doctrine basically says that having a higher purpose for the land than its current occupants gives the holder of that higher purpose the duty and justification to take the land by whatever means necessary to fulfill the higher purpose. Public interest is now the assumed justification propelling the environmental plutocrats' purported higher purpose for the land. Though manifest destiny and public trust rationale had very different philosophical roots, they certainly appear to have crossed paths.

Looking at the broad history of land takings from the colonial period to the present, the power invoked in the name of public good essentially replaced manifest destiny doctrine. There is a fuzzy period in the late 1800's, in the early Indian Allotment and Assimilation Policy period, where you can see the blending of manifest destiny thinking with public interest rationale. Then of course, after it was no longer politically advisable to use manifest destiny rhetoric, public good rhetoric replaces it entirely.

As soon as the federal government conquered Indian America all the way to the Pacific, it initiated a second campaign of conquest with the public interest rationale. This campaign for land, water and natural resources began with the establishment of the National Parks system, promoted to the public as conservation and economic stimulation through nature tourism, and many public works projects promoted as cures for the economic destruction of the Great Depression. The privileged class that pursues this *still ongoing* campaign of apparent rural economic conquest continue to justify their actions with public interest, and public trust rationale.

It is, in effect, the *second wave of manifest destiny now turned against the whole public*. This political and economic conquest is what insightful, outspoken Indians from Russell Means (Lakota) to Elwood Mose (Te-Moak Western Shoshone) seem to allude to when they say that the American public are now the "new Indians". If the rural public as a whole is to avoid the tragic potential of this second wave of manifest destiny, in today's globalization reality, we will certainly need to achieve the unity that once eluded Tecumseh.

Thus the public needs to resolve its conflicts over government's overlapping promises to them. If not, if we remain divided, changing interpretation of the Public Trust Doctrine - along with environmental laws, international agreements and a lot of help from the rich - will incrementally wipe-out all notion of rural Indian and non-Indian local self-determination. Along with that will go the social and economic security of land-based and, consequently, urban peoples in the US. With that will also go the hope of human rights and self-determination for land-based peoples that the US Constitution, and the more lofty side of the American Revolution, once promised to display to the world.

The more you peek into this Pandora's box, the more disturbing it gets. National Parks and public works projects were promoted by the industrial and political-economic elite of the early 20th Century as conservation, nature tourism economics and general economic recovery in the name of the greater public good. Today we hear that same familiar ring in the enviro-economic political arena.

These early ambitious projects promoted in the name of greater public good also gave the dominant society the perfect excuse to eliminate off-reservation Indian settlements and "hillbilly" communities in the mountains and remote places. Both communities were peoples whose existence and cultures disturbed the dominant society that considered itself superior, more civilized in all things. Many openly loathed and feared them. Allotment and Termination policy, too, was essentially excused as a public interest issue, claiming that the tribes had excess land that was needed more by the whole public. These notions, too, should all have a familiar ring in today's enviro-economic politics and it's anti-rural lifestyle rhetoric.

Today the tribes are trying to recover from a long trail of broken treaties and regain or settle the property rights that were promised to them. This is *propelled by an overwhelming need for economic development*, a need to rise out of the historical poverty and dispossession in Indian country. At the same time, non-Indian rural America is facing waves of regulatory and market induced socioeconomic damage, *also in need of economic development*. This sometimes results in a legal tug-of-war between overlapping rights to natural resources promised to tribes and settlers, resources necessary to both communities' socioeconomic survival.

As if this situation is not contentious enough, enter the era of environmental law. It is not that we do not need environmental preservation or protection - *we certainly do* - but there is the matter of— *who controls that?* Will globally operating corporate conglomerates or small rural communities, both Indian and non-Indian, end up on top after the economic fallout? Will there be room for both? So far, small business and the land-based rural communities it supports are losing to the big guys.

Will all this socioeconomic sacrifice forced on the non-elite rural class prevent global super-industries from polluting with impunity, or guarantee that they treat the little people well? So far, as any average watcher of the news can plainly see, that obviously doesn't look good either.

Although public trust rationale has often been elevated over non-Indian prior rights, neither the federal government nor the tribes have pushed a case that pits public trust doctrine, involving the Endangered Species Act for example, versus tribal treaty rights. So far, they have been able to resolve conflict outside the courtroom with cooperative agreements, memorandums of agreement and understanding, and other government-to-government agreements.

However, this may not hold for long, if, for instance, a well-financed environmental coalition files suit against a tribe under an environmental law or international environmental treaty or agreement as a public trust issue. That may just break the dam, so to speak, with the courts deciding that environmental laws or agreements are a public trust issue that supersede Indian treaty rights.

Since this country uses case law, such a precedent will open up tribal rights to the possibility of being snuffed with public trust issues every time a conflict arises in a public trust venue. That could happen in the case of opposition to Makah whale hunting, or it might be something just down the road like wild salmon campaigns that oppose hatcheries or wilderness campaigns that op-

pose virtually all human use of the land, water and its natural resources. Given the profoundly anti-human and anti-Indian con-
viction already within deep ecology, animal rights and wilderness
environmental organizations, it is bound to happen sooner or later.

I presented these general concerns, and an April 26, 2002 news
quote from LA Times relating to the Klamath Basin, Oregon, water conflict, to the Klamath Tribes' water attorney, Carl Ullman. I
thank him for his candid reply. In the basin, water rights for domestic use, farm irrigation, other non-farm business uses, tribal
treaty rights to fisheries and food gathering, and ESA demands
for water for listed fish species, all converge in the same watershed.

The news quote I referred to read, "A 1995 federal solicitor's
opinion states that endangered species get priority for water in the
basin, followed by Indian tribes who fish for salmon and then by
irrigators who supply the farmers". The federal solicitor cited
said the tribes' prior reserved treaty rights, which date to time
immemorial, *follow* the ESA in priority. Below is the comment
made by the tribal water attorney:

"The underlying question whether the ESA gets priority over Indian treaty rights is one on which both the feds and the Tribes
have avoided seeking a direct answer. So the law is not really
clear. Apparently neither side wants to test the various theories,
some of which are alluded to in your message to me. So far as I
know, thus far the parties have been able to resolve whatever
issues arose short of litigation. The Makah whaling issue may be
an exception. I don't know as much about that as I should."

Back on November 8, 2000, a letter to NOAA from former Makah
Tribal Council Chairman, Ben Johnson, Jr., states: "The Tribal
Council has been committed to working cooperatively with the
United States government to develop protocols which allow the
Tribe to implement its treaty whaling rights, while allowing the
government to meet its other domestic and international obligations. This policy of cooperation is not without controversy within
the Tribe, however. Your unilateral decision to rescind the cooperative agreement, and NMFS's delay in completing the NEPA

process increases the pressure on the Tribal Council to explore other options for implementing the Tribe's whaling rights."

Though the difficulty referred to in Johnson's letter was subsequently resolved, it is important to note that the Makah signed a cooperative agreement with federal agencies which the agencies obviously felt they could unilaterally rescind. That could certainly cause some doubt within the tribe about the reliability of agency cooperation, which could go a long way to explaining why that cooperation was not without controversy within the tribe. The cooperative agreement served to shield the tribe's treaty right to hunt whale from other international agreements and treaties that might otherwise be interpreted as a conflicting public trust issue.

The courts and federal agencies have upheld the Makah tribe's treaty right to hunt non-ESA listed whale. However, what realistic options to US courts and federal agency cooperative agreements the tribe would have is difficult to pinpoint. If US courts and federal agencies do not, for some reason, continue to support the Makah's right in the future, who will? The UN? That may not be reliable. The US with whom the tribes have a trust relationship, has signed international agreements concerning whales.

Even if the UN recognized the tribes as nations, it may take the stance that its recognition of Indian tribes' nationhood does not require UN honoring of treaty rights granted not by them, but by the US, if they interfere with International Law. The whole point of developing international law is to establish law that supersedes and presumably corrects those of individual sovereign nations that might otherwise have sufficiently compelling reason to resist compliance. It is profoundly obvious that such an arrangement does not exist simply to cheerfully accommodate dissenting sovereigns' positions.

The anti-whaling faction certainly appears to be picking at the edges of these issues in the case of the Makah whalers. After the long and controversial legal battles that finally led to the first Makah hunt in 70 years, in 1999, environmental opposition succeeded in obtaining a temporary restraining order from the court to hold back a second hunt, on May 3, 2002. This move, they hoped, would prevent the hunt until their main lawsuit is decided in the courts. However, further restraining orders were subsequently denied by the court on May 17, and the Bush administration continues to uphold the Makah whaling right.

Yet the battle to defeat the Makah treaty property right to hunt whale continues unabated. Perhaps most thought-provoking is that the extreme environmentalist-oriented anti-Makah whaling faction is joined by a minority number of typically non-environmental group elements and conservative politicians Jack Metcalf and Slade Gorton. Here is an anti-Indian treaty rights stance that tends to originate in response to government's overlapping promises, jurisdictional property disputes, conflicting industry interests or Indian gaming issues.

So, mixed in among groups that oppose the Makah, like the Humane Society, PETA, Sea Shepherd and Ocean Defense International, are visible and perhaps also discreet elements that may hope to defeat treaty rights for entirely different political and financial reasons.

This is a rather unusual combination, to say the least. Conservative elements can normally be expected to support property rights and to defend the right to responsibly hunt non-ESA species. In point of fact, some think tanks and organizations that are perceived as conservative, like Junkscience.com and Capital Research Center's Green-Watch have publicly posted reports favorable to the Makah right to hunt whale. This is a consistent sovereignty-oriented and sound science stance.

Yet an ill-advised right-left anti-treaty rights or anti-sovereignty environmental coalition fighting the Makah hunt or some similar treaty right, however small in numbers or marginal in overall political compatibility, could nevertheless ultimately destroy Indian *and* non-Indian natural resource property rights with public trust rationale and domestic environmental or international law in one disastrous blow.

The socio-economic welfare of both Indian and non-Indian land-based communities that depend on local sovereignty and prior reserved rights would be laid completely bare to those with the deep pockets necessary for filing more such lawsuits. This obviously is not where forward-looking Indian rights and sovereignty supporters, nor non-Indian rural rights supporters, want to go.

On another more far reaching front, wild salmon coalitions would like to take wild salmon recovery issues to court as a public trust issue. They assert that salmon hatchery programs (including tribal hatcheries) and multiple management and jurisdiction (including tribal management and jurisdiction) both threaten wild salmon recovery.

Wild salmon proponents rationalize that wild salmon should be viewed as both *a public amenity and a public inheritance*, fulfilling a biological diversity function and a sort of 'spiritual aesthetics of the wild' ethos. This, they believe, should *replace* the traditional public interest view of salmon as both *a biologically desirable, essential wildlife and food species*.

This milieu asserts we should prevent fishing of certain abundant runs of hatchery-born salmon if they contain even relatively minute mixing with instream-born "wild" fish. They aim to outlaw fish hatcheries in all but those cases where they are the only way to preserve or replace a specific wild fish population. Wild salmon proponents speak in terms of changing patterns, and changing *cultures*.

They seek to culturally redefine wild salmon as an inherited public amenity of much greater social, economic and biological importance than abundant free running salmon as a public food source. Essentially, they demonize the abundant hatchery salmon food source as the dastardly cattle of the sea. The entire spectrum of the wilderness-oriented milieu's lack of concern for feeding humans, in fact, is quite staggering when viewed collectively.

There are obvious threats in this wild salmon rationale for non-Indian fishing communities, tribal fishing communities, and the local socioeconomic sovereignty of Indian and non-Indian rural communities affected in general by salmon recovery policy. This chapter will later explore the wild salmon as public trust rationale from papers underwritten by the Bullitt Foundation, based in Seattle, WA, which is founded on the Bullitt family's considerable industry wealth.

A third far-reaching front involves the wilderness movement that has, indeed, moved— all the way to the oceans. The "Ocean Wilderness" movement arrived with its own science theorists, enviro-political coalitions, web sites, networks, big campaigns and really big foundation funding. Its legal strategies for designating wilderness areas in the oceans are already developed.

The Gulf of Maine International Wilderness web page titled "How do we designate 'Ocean Wilderness'?" lays it out quite dryly—

"(1) Pursuant to the President's 5/26/00 Marine Protected Areas Proclamation. Read the May 26, 2000 press briefing about the new joint Interior/NOAA marine protected area program. (2) Pursuant to that proclamation, by enacting designation under one or more of these protected area management programs that are under the Interior Department's jurisdiction. (3) As a Marine National Monument? Justice Department says *Presidents can do so.* *How does the Prime Minister designate the Canadian half of the Ocean Wilderness? Pursuant to the Canada Oceans Act, which empowers the Prime Minister, with the assent of at least two cabinet ministers, to declare a Marine Protected Area designation. How can the US/Canada joint ocean wilderness declaration be carried out? (1)Pursuant to the 'Shared Border Accords of 1995' signed by President Clinton and Prime Minister Chretien. Read about the Accords in the October 1999, 'Joint US/Canada Statement on Border Cooperation' Or (2) By the same type of agreement that was signed in 1964 by President Lyndon B. Johnson of the United States and Prime Minister Lester B. Pearson of Canada, to designate the Roosevelt/Campobello Island International Park on the Maine/New Brunswick Border (in New Brunswick) or (3) As an International Peace Park, similar to Waterton/Glacier International Peace Park"

Much of the groundwork was laid for this during the Clinton administration. A Clinton administration federal research document on legal devises for proclaiming various forms of marine wilderness titled "Marine National Monuments & Marine National Wildlife Refuges, A US Department of Justice report on applying the Antiquities Act & the National Wildlife Refuge Act to marine habitat and wildlife protection in federal and EEZ waters. Dated September 15, 2000" can be viewed at http://www.atlantisforce.org/doj1.html .

Although the document is too lengthy to include here, among the many thought-provoking statements in the report, are: "Although the public trust doctrine....might limit in some ways the extent of the Government's control over the territorial sea....the Government nonetheless maintains ample room under the doctrine to exercise dominion over that area to protect it and its resources for public enjoyment."

Got that? Pubic "enjoyment" is their concern here, not food. It goes on: "Moreover, the creation of a national monument to protect living marine resources would be consistent with the Government's role as public trustee....In our view, then, because the territorial sea is subject to the sovereignty of the United States, Congress may regulate it under the Property Clause."

The federal report ends: "We have concluded that the President may establish a national monument pursuant to the Antiquities Act in both the territorial sea and the EEZ....With respect to management issues, we find that authority to manage monuments can, under certain circumstances, be shared between the Department of the Interior and other agencies, that the FWS must maintain sole management authority over any national wildlife refuge area within a monument, that regulations applicable to national monuments trump inconsistent fishery management plans, and that the establishment of a national monument would not preclude the establishment of a national marine sanctuary in the same area."

It bears repeating, with emphasis added—
·   US Fish & Wildlife Service "*must* maintain *sole* management authority over any national wildlife refuge area within a monument"
·   "regulations applicable to national monuments *trump inconsistent fishery management plans*"

"establishment of a national monument *would not preclude* the establishment of a national marine sanctuary *in the same area*"

A University of Oregon web system page titled "State Public Trust Authority and Federal And State Navigation Servitudes: Class #3" outlines how public trust doctrine can be applied to environmental law. It also explains that even though the US is not a party, claiming specific exceptions, to UNCLOS, the United Nations Convention on the Law of the Sea, it is "[v]iewed as a codification of customary IL [International Law] and thus is binding on even non parties. The Ocean is the Rugged Edge of Sovereignty - where the sovereign authority of a co[a]stal state becomes less as it moves away from land."

Ocean wilderness campaigns plan to take advantage of that 'rugged edge of sovereignty' where the coastal state's sovereign authority purportedly diminishes as it moves away from land. Federal as well as state or tribal sovereigns' "inconsistent fisheries management plans" are what the ocean wildlanders seek to circumvent, along with their very sovereignty.

The environmental industry's wilderness campaign cannot reasonably be expected to be any less anti-human in its demands for the less privileged class to sacrifice its needs on the ocean, nor any less anti-self-determination, than it already has been as *it* moves away from land. We should recall that wilderness proponents on land have suggested anywhere from 50% to 95% percent of the US land mass must immediately or eventually be designated wilderness and wilderness corridor in order for human civilization, as they see it, to be sustainable.

Wildlanders envision barring virtually all users access to this vast continental wilderness, except approved government and NGO scientific observers, and those few members of the public well funded and physically unchallenged enough for rugged hiking, and possibly cross-country skiing and snow-shoeing excursions. If you know the right people and are somehow immune to the law, you can take a chopper in at your convenience. High level bureaucrats like former Secretary of the Interior, Bruce Babbitt, apparently qualify for these kinds of perks.

Yet the non-elite public are to believe that this is not a non-democratic, socioeconomically discriminatory elitist idea, but a wholly benevolent and necessary mandate for mutual sacrifice by the less privileged for our own good.

The wilderness movement's extensive land and water acquisition or control goals are wrapped in the warm, fuzzy garb of public trust rhetoric. Yet broad public acceptance of this concept would move the likelihood of far too many small communities' survival in the rural and coastal landscape from threatened to endangered to extinction. We can't all expect to survive as remote little tourist attractions for the rich, nor as road-eradication labor for the wildlanders. This, too, is not where forward-thinking Indian rights and sovereignty supporters, nor non-Indian rural rights supporters, want to go.

Yet this is the sobering picture in today's rural landscape. The likely future terrain looks like Indian and non-Indian rural communities should strive to support each others' rights and work out any conflicts, so that they can both protect their welfare in greater numbers. However, old obstacles to cooperation remain that derive from US society's history, years of polarity, enmity or obvious misunderstanding, and the very nature of divide and conquer as a political reality itself.

This is a very important human rights concern. A picture emerges in which, in the long run, as land-based communities remain divided against each other, corporate and foundation funded environmental lawsuits that are largely restrictive and punitive to small rural communities will steadily break the socioeconomic vitality and flexibility of these communities. Astoundingly, we won't even have saved the environment in the process. We will have simply advanced globalization, essentially an elite funded and directed re-colonization of the entire planet.

It is both surprising and incriminating that widely read journalists like Knudsen and environmentalists like Tokar and Dowie research and expose the plutocratic nature of modern environmentalism, yet nobody in the environmental community seems to be making any truly relevant adjustments. In this slick media-polarized nature versus man venue, if natural resource users point it out, they are simply ignored, smeared as secret big industry shills or belittled as conspiracy nuts, thus their voice is successfully labeled and marginalized. The polarization and division on many fronts seems to be getting worse.

In recent years we have seen a handful of organizations like CERA and Upstate Citizens for Equality, and some politicians claiming to support property rights who have taken on an anti-Indian sovereignty tone. A relatively small group of dissatisfied non-Indian property owners whose lands fall within reservation boundaries and jurisdiction have long been the core of these organizations. The related 'equal rights for red and white' sloganeers focus on seeking to eliminate treaty rights rather than effectively promoting fulfillment of equal rights.

These people, quite ill-advisedly, I should emphasize, believe that assaulting treaty rights or tribal sovereignty will solve their complaints. Yet the majority of the public who support property rights have a bone to pick with state or federal agencies and big name environmental coalitions, rather than the tribes.

At the same time, we have more conflicts steadily cropping up over use of sacred sites, land, water, fish, soil, minerals, oil, grasslands, shorelines, roads, trails and just about every other aspect of rural life you can think of. All the while, the deep ecology - wilderness - animal rights wing pushes the envelope to define humans as alien to the natural world, having virtually no positive role to play in a healthy wild environment. Social ecologists have pointed out how dismally anti-human the deep ecology movement is.

Those perceived as more mainstream environmental organizations compound the negative situation because they tend to push wedge issues that get between Indian and non-Indian communities. Yet after such coalitions get what they want, they typically fail to actually support Indian issues like land-base acquisition, resource harvest, toxics clean-up, and so on. These coalitions cite treaty fishing rights when they sue for water under the ESA, but whether they sincerely support tribal rights to realistic *food fisheries* is an entirely different matter.

A prominent player in the Klamath Basin water rights conflict, Pacific Coast Federation of Fishermen's Associations (PCFFA) is a frequent signer on water for fish lawsuits, and particularly what some are calling fish versus farm suits. This organization's leaders submit testimony from the Potomac to the Pacific expressing grave concern for Pacific coast commercial fishing communities and also claim to be the largest such fishing association. However, some commercial fishermen on the Washington coast report that PCFFA doesn't really represent the majority of Pacific coast commercial fishermen.

According to some members of the Puget Sound Gillnetters Association (PSGA), a number of fishermen that used to support PCFFA have dropped that support because they surmised that the organization was using them as 'harmed parties' in its campaigns with other environmental groups, but somehow failing to oppose closures on fisheries important to the very fishermen it claims to represent. Port Townsend, WA, PSGA local's president, Chris Stoess, estimates that PCFFA may only represent as few as 20% of Pacific coast fishermen. Ocean wilderness campaigns can't be lurking too far away in the historically vast and murky waters of fish politics.

Meanwhile, inland wild salmon groups bash hatcheries, and agency biologists in Oregon and Washington literally bash thousands of hatchery born salmon per year to death with clubs. These are healthy salmon that have survived and returned from rigorous years in the ocean, to finally spawn in the wild. Salmon clubbing has been documented on film in the Alsea Valley in Oregon and taken to court by both Indian and non-Indian parties. It is an obviously wasteful genetic cleansing regime that is opposed and protested by both rural Indian and non-Indian communities in both states. In Washington, the Colvilles and Yakimas oppose the same activity in the Methow Valley along non-Indian rural residents.

However, no environmentalists in flashy salmon suits have turned-
out to defend these fish, as they did to rally for breaching Northwest dams, even though no genetic difference can be found between hatchery and wild fish. Instead, tribal members, local non-
Indian residents and even conservative Washington state sena-
tors Bob Morton and Harold Hochstatter scrambled in the river
trapping fish to keep them away from the fisheries management
agency's clubs. It seems apparent that the hatcheries have been
too successful for the environmental coalitions that focus their
vast resources on eliminating humans and human activity from
the natural world.

PSGA fishermen tell head spinning tales about state and federal
fish agencies actually working to cause salmon shortages since
the 1940's. It is basically portrayed as a combination of guaranteed job security and big operating budgets for the agencies, a bit
of outright corruption, and essentially a keep-the-crisis-going-be-
cause-it-pays scenario.

They say that some fish agency personnel were making illegal
salmon egg sales to Chile and other foreign countries for decades,
building up foreign fisheries while tearing ours down. Fishermen,
and even marginalized biologists, claim there are very simple, effective in-stream salmon recovery schemes available that the agencies refuse to use. Fishermen claim that government fisheries
agents have sometimes even stolen their fish or equipment right
off their fishing boats.

The documents these gillnetters hoped would provide evidence of
such charges in court are now reportedly gathering dust in storage at a Washington university, because they simply ran out of
financial resources to sue. Their two most respected leaders were
apparently murdered on their own fishing boats. The whole story
seems something that bears serious investigation. Yet no one seems
forthcoming with the resources required to cover legal staff time,
to have a look at these documents. The gillnetters were effectively demonized, marginalized and discarded years ago.

I was surprised to be informed by Stoess that National Marine
Fisheries Service funding is based on how much seafood the US

imports, not how much domestic fisheries abundance they can produce. That seems a bit of a dis-incentive. Who besides bureaucrats might benefit? Big foreign fishing fleets, large corporate investors in fish and other seafood farms producing cheap fare for human consumption, and sport fishing industry interests which often advocate the closure of commercial fisheries, might all benefit. Small commercial fishers seem to lose every which way.

So, when PCFFA sues along with other environmental groups, demanding more water for ESA listed fish, I don't jump for joy for fishermen, because the fishermen are likely to lose even if PCFFA wins. PSGA is just one commercial fishermen's group that pulled their support for PCFFA. Some time after PSGA made that decision, Stoess toured the Klamath Basin on the Oregon-California border in the summer of 2001 to see for himself the devastating results of the water shut-off to 1,400 basin farm families and refuge wildlife that resulted from a PCFFA environmental group coalition lawsuit demanding more water for ESA listed fish.

As a result of the damage to farms and refuge wildlife Stoess witnessed, PSGA posted an apology on the web for their part in the lawsuit, which was initiated prior to PSGA's disassociation with PCFFA. Putting farmers and wildlife in jeopardy was not what PSGA intended or expected. Stoess reported that PSGA was trying to have its name removed from a PCFFA suit. However, PCFFA continues to sue along with other foundation-funded environmental organizations.

Currently, the Klamath Tribes, who have treaty guaranteed fishing, hunting and gathering rights in the basin, basin farm irrigation agencies and relevant government agency appointees are engaged in a Bush administration-mandated cooperative team effort to resolve the Basin's water conflicts and environmental problems.

However, news reports on a subsequent April 2002 lawsuit alleging that planned irrigation operations of the basin's Klamath Project will harm fish even in this non-drought year, read as though Indian tribes were part of the suit, when in fact they were not. The suit was, in fact, filed by PCFFA, Institute for Fisheries Resources,

Oregon Natural Resource Council, Klamath Forest Alliance, Northcoast Environmental Center, WaterWatch Oregon and Defenders of Wildlife.

Quite frequently environmental organizations tout Indian rights in their public relations material, often giving the impression that they are somehow associated with the tribes. When news releases either falsely imply or assume that the tribes are part of a suit or an association, it causes basin farmers to fear that the tribes may not really negotiate with them.

Perhaps a history of these kinds of actions may have contributed to the Klamath County Commissioners decision to give county funds to a private group filing another lawsuit it hopes will redefine the Klamath Tribes' now senior water rights. Perhaps this kind of tactic dampened the growing enthusiasm some farm supporters had held for the possibility that their support for the Klamath Tribes' land acquisition proposal might result in a successful cooperative venture between the tribes and the farmers.

AP reported, May 8, 2002: "The Klamath County Board of Commissioners has allocated $50,000 in county money to help farmers appeal a recent court ruling they say unfairly favors the Klamath Tribes. The funds, which will come out of the county's risk management fund, will go to the nonprofit group Resource Conservancy, which represents Upper Klamath Basin farmers and ranchers appealing the ruling."

Resource Conservancy is a private organization that represents individual basin farmers who are members, as opposed to representing an entire irrigation district, or all the districts in the basin. The tribes stress that their rights have been repeatedly affirmed in court and object that this may not be an appropriate use of county funds. It appears there may yet be a long road ahead, not only to returning to the cooperative efforts that were underway in the basin before that controversial summer of 2001, but to the cooperation that President Bush has now mandated.

At the same time, when farmers get water before all matters are finally settled, the tribes must entertain fears that the farmers will think they have no need to negotiate with the them. So far, in this new Bush-mandated negotiating process, the Klamath Tribes have refrained from filing suit against the Klamath Project. The Tribes are encouraged that Secretary of the Interior, Gail Norton, has recognized the tribes' water rights as property rights, and that she has put their proposal for a much needed land base on the table for discussion. The tribes hope to regain a portion of their lost reservation that is now part of the Winema National Forest.

In March 2002, when Secretary Norton presided over the release of spring's first irrigation water to the Klamath Project farmers, it was, of course a happy occasion for them, which Klamath tribal chairman, Alan Foreman, came to observe. The Tribes' formal press release on the event says: "'We are happy for the people who are getting water,' said Klamath Tribal Chairman Allen Foreman. 'But while the headgates are opening and the farmers are returning to their fields, our fisheries remain closed and our livelihoods compromised. Justice will be served only when both we and the farmers can return to our livelihoods.'"

However, a small group of non-Klamath native protesters, and non-Indian environmental protesters in the usual fish suits, also attended, conducting a reportedly loud protest. Unfortunately, the average observer did not know these protesters were not Klamath tribal members. This kind of activity, too, can add to polarity or misunderstanding in a situation that is already quite complex, in which two communities' welfare is at stake.

Meanwhile, a number of key basin irrigator supporters have also expressed support for the Tribes' land-base acquisition for quite some time, long before the water shut-off of 2001. An October 5, 1999 Associated Press report titled *Land Give Back* reads:

"'We believe that the pieces to construct a comprehensive solution are in place, and miraculously the pieces could benefit practically every interest,' said Marshall Staunton, a farmer and member of the Tulelake Growers, which drafted the plan....The tribe's 45-year quest to regain its reservation has gained support from key members of the agricultural community, surprising many area residents....Supporters praised the tribe's efforts to resolve water issues outside of courtrooms and condemned the 1954 federal taking of the timber-rich reservation....The tribe has 'done an excellent job to bring the parties to the table and sit down to talk about some very delicate issues,' said irrigator Mike McKoen of Merrill. 'I think they have a legitimate claim there, and I think it would benefit the economy of the entire region,' added Earl Miller of Bonanza."

Have any of the suing environmental groups expressed support for the Tribes to acquire the land base they need? *No.* Not one official endorsement to date. That is not what the environmental industry does.

The Klamath Tribes plan to manage their intended forest land acquisition for sustainable timber harvest. The Klamaths believe they can manage the forest land better than the Forest Service has, and in a manner that will result in more water availability in the Klamath watershed for both fish and farms. Foreman says the Tribes' would be willing to pay the cash-strapped counties a share of timber receipts so that the tribes' gain is not simply a loss in similar Forest Service payments for the counties. This is a win-win situation for the Klamath Tribes and the farmers.

However, the Tribes' land acquisition proposal is not the sort of thing the environmental industry approves of. Instead, it has a history of opposing tribes that try to regain land they have lost to federal agencies. Native American Rights fund stated on their web site, January 4, 2002: "The Tribes are continuing their face-to-face discussion with leaders of the conservation community, led by the Wilderness Society, concerning any condition that would be a part of the transfer of National forest lands to the Tribes." Yet no support from any of these environmental groups has been announced.

The Wilderness Society's web site states: "A Coalition for the Klamath Basin is a new alliance [1997] of local, regional, and national organizations dedicated to conserving and restoring the Klamath Basin. Founding members of this new coalition include The Wilderness Society, Klamath Basin Audubon Society, Klamath Forest Alliance, Oregon Natural Resources Council, Pacific

Coast Federation of Fishermen's Associations, Institute for Fisheries Resources, Sierra Club-Oregon Chapter, and Water Watch. The coalition has prepared A Conservation Vision for the Klamath Basin and have pledged to work together to promote and implement the vision and actions presented in this document."

These well-funded, litigious organizations have pledged, it says, to work together to promote and implement *their vision* for the basin. They have made no such pledge to the farmers' *or* the Tribes'. Nor are the likely to. They are paid to implement the environmental industry's vision. Their lives and futures are not dependent on a fair and equitable arrangement in the basin, as the Tribes' and the farmers' lives are.

In *Klamath Tribes seeks part of forest*, the *Oregonian*'s Courtney Thompson reports, all the way back in December 14, 1999: "But the little-understood history of the tribes, combined with a struggle over water rights and endangered species, will make the tribes' task difficult....Environmental groups don't want to lose their ability to appeal sales on the public forest if it becomes tribal trust land."

The closest thing to an environmental group stating a position on this, that I have been able to find in the media, is an AP report dated January 31, 2000, posted on *Oregon Live*. It read—

"The tribes are seeking to regain a portion of their homeland, which includes much of the Winema National Forest. They presented their 100-year sustainability strategy for that land to the Ashland-based Headwaters environmental group on Friday....'I thought it was very successful, very professional', Headwaters board member Mary-Kay Michelsen said of the presentation.... But she cautioned that the board has not taken an official position."

The presentation was merely complimented by Headwaters as "professional", but no "official position" taken. That's a far cry from endorsement.

The Klamath Tribes have expressed concern for the 1,400 or so farms that were harmed by BOR's irrigation shut-off in the summer of 2001, as well as concern for their own tribal community. They issued an official water update at the outset of the summer to clarify their position on the Interior Department's management plan that called for the shut-off. It said, in part—

"That Interior management plan has triggered much anger in the farming community. As you have seen, the Klamath Tribes have not been fairly represented in the local newspaper, which continues to confuse our own tribal membership and the general public. Therefore, the following information has been prepared by the Klamath Tribes, in hopes to shed some light on this major crisis situation."

The statement went on, in part, to say: "We also believe the federal government has a responsibility to the farm families who, like the Klamath Tribes, now depend on a water system that is simply not capable of meeting current demands. We as a people, who for years have felt the pain of being unable to meet the needs of our families and communities, do not want to see our friends and neighbors in the agriculture community suffer….Not surprisingly the current crises is a predictable result of the federal government making more promises than it can keep….Those of us who must face the consequences of those empty promises cannot build a future by turning on each other. The fisheries, the farming communities, the Klamath Tribes culture and economy are all at risk."

Later that summer, when Upper Klamath Lake was discovered to contain excess water, Secretary Norton released a modest amount of irrigation water to the farms. The Tribes' response on July 24, 2001 said: "Today's announcement by the Secretary of the Interior is welcome news for our distressed region. As long as the release of water does not jeopardize the fish and eco-systems that are so important to the culture and livelihood of The Klamath Tribes and the wellness of the entire Klamath basin- we support using surplus water for farming purposes….We empathize with farmers who, like us, were made a promise by the federal government that was not fulfilled."

However, the environmental industry's rhetoric on agriculture historically ranges from theory-based, intellectual posturing to downright callous, unsympathetic blaming. It strikes me as bizarre that these folks justify their own food consumption. The fact of the matter is, that it is the small family farms, ranches and orchards that still have the capability of producing a very varied food supply, that are being incrementally wiped-out by the pressures and train-wrecks of enviro-economic globalization.

Continuing to eliminate by financially fatal regulation or even buying out clusters of remaining small farm operations is certainly not going to turn this bad trend around. It has been going on for decades now. More federal farm land acquisition bills and global market pressures don't make the prospects look good for small farm recovery. The family farm, too, is truly endangered. People who are sincere about the environment should also ask themselves, who's going to grow their food when they vote the family farm away?

It is not hard to tell real land-based people from distanced, theoretical elitists in this kind of scenario. Do you see the mess I see? It's a classic divide and conquer scenario. Abundant hatchery salmon runs that feed people are characterized by environmentalism as the evil cattle of the ocean. Yet inland, cows and farmers are accused of killing the fish. Sheep and pigs are in the doghouse, too. Orchards in the Methow Valley, same place they club hatchery salmon, are being torn out to make more water for salmon. Doesn't this all seem a bit perverse? It seems to me that much of humanity's food sources are being outlawed. They are either being eliminated on both land and water, or are being narrowly focused toward globalized agribusiness in a manner which is not very wise.

Tribal and independent fishermen, and family farmers are all losing their livelihoods at a steady pace. Their small communities are economically distressed to the point of endangerment. There's something wrong with this picture. This is what decades of federal management and environmental lawsuits has produced! This highly politicized system of litigious conflict and central regulation is certainly not working well for these small communities.

The Klamath Basin could be a grand opportunity for an Indian and non-Indian community to resolve a really sticky mess that big government created. Joint research in pursuit of sound management science by a community's real on-the-ground stakeholders, when grounded by a scientifically solid program, can achieve great success through its superior ability to innovate and adapt to the area's unique characteristics. The Klamath Basin farmers, real commercial fishermen and the Klamath Tribes could solve the basin's conflict and its environmental problems if they were really empowered to do so.

This is how the damages wrought by centralized management and misguided politicized scientific theory could be reversed. This is far more compatible with local self-determination. The added motivation of the real hands-on stakeholders to resolve all challenges to the community's best interests provides fuel for creative problem-solving.

However, we don't know if the well-financed environmental industry players that thrive and advance on conflict within the landscape will ever let that happen. Such conflicts are enough to resolve without outside influences that benefit in some fashion by keeping the conflict alive, or even escalating it. Division and enmity are fatal to gaining or retaining local self-determination. Some tempers in the basin have allegedly flared out of hand. On reading these accounts, one is reminded of Debra Callahan's EGA divide and neutralize speech.

There was an alcohol-related drive through sign-and-outhouse shooting spree involving racist rhetoric, shouting "sucker lovers", as three young basin area men careened through a small basin town. The incident took place in Chiloquin, a town of mostly Klamath tribal members. Fortunately, there were no injuries. The case is reportedly being prosecuted.

Environmentalist Felice Pace, founder of the Klamath Forest Alliance, reports the Pioneer Press on April 2002, has been accused of assaulting former Alliance employee, James McCarthy. The news source also reported: "This is not the first time that there has been a complaint of battery against Felice Pace. In September the Yreka Police Department filed a case with the district attorney regarding an alleged battery by Pace against Karuk Tribal Council member, Frank Woods."

Klamath Forest Alliance is active in environmental campaigns and legal actions throughout the greater Klamath Basin region, including the lawsuits affecting the Klamath irrigation project. One certainly wonders what may have inspired Pace to assault a Karuk tribal council member.

It should also provoke concern that the upstream water users in the Klamath watershed have not been made to contribute water for the two, now famous, species of ESA listed sucker fish. Also troublesome is that hydropower dams have not been successfully addressed in terms of their role in the solution to the Klamath Project conflict.

This concern is reflected in the Bureau of Reclamation's comments to NMFS and USF&W on the agencies' most recent biological opinion on the Klamath Project, reported in the Herald and News on June 4, 2002 by Ryan Harper. "The letters also take issue with the burden of responsibility placed upon the Bureau by the two agencies. According to Rodgers, the Bureau is being asked to control factors beyond the range of the project, including such things as flows through PacifiCorp dams and water quality problems at the upper end of Klamath Lake."

On March 20, 2002, Herald and News' Anita Burke reported: "PacifiCorp announced Tuesday it is prepared to go to court to block any attempt by the U.S. Fish and Wildlife Service to force the power company to install fish screens on its Link River hydro diversion....PacifiCorp said it fears the biological opinion due out in a few weeks will call for fish screens on its two small hydroelectric diversions at the Link River Dam....The U.S. Bureau of Reclamation's biological assessment of project operations called for installing screens on the nearby A Canal headworks to prevent fish from being sucked into the irrigation canal system....By sending out a notice of intent to sue in 60 days, the utility wanted to encourage the Fish and Wildlife Service to open discussions with the company and possibly initiate changes in its biological opinion...."

Oregon Natural Resource Council responded: "It is somewhat remarkable that PacifiCorp has sent a 60 day notice of intent to sue USFWS....Exactly a year ago ONRC and Klamath Forest Alliance filed a lawsuit demanding the screens as BOR had not fulfilled its obligations as required by other prior BiOps to install these screens."

Going back to November 2, 2001, Burke also reported under the headline *Congress OK's fish screens*: "The Energy and Water Development Act allocates $15 million for operations of the Klamath Reclamation Project, including $5 million for construction of a fish screen on the A Canal....The U.S. Fish and Wildlife Service has said a fish screen is an important step in protecting sucker fish in Upper Klamath Lake."

Oregon's Representative Greg Walden agreed, "Providing funds for the construction of a fish screen on the A Canal is another positive step toward resolving the crisis that exists in the Klamath Basin." Money has been allocated, and yet PacifiCorp balks at the expense of doing its part to protect the ESA listed sucker fish while headlines and environmental coalitions continue to pit the Klamath Project farmers and the Klamath Tribes against each other for precious water.

On the hydropower giant's profit end, Seth Zuckerman wrote an April 8, 2001 environmental piece, posted on Tidepool, titled "Follow the Water". He reports that PacifiCorp was positioned to reap estimated total financial benefits of $2.5 to $7 million from the water shut off of Klamath Basin farmers, depending upon how electric rates played out that summer of 2001. PacifiCorp, owning numerous hydropower dams throughout the Northwest, is itself owned by the Britain-based transnational power behemoth, Scottish Power.

Klamath Basin resident, Carmen Bair, and her husband, John, operate an organic dairy. She reports that PacifiCorp was in charge of reading lake levels on the Klamath Project's water storage lake that summer. Carmen reports that after independent parties surveyed the lake level, found it to be one foot higher than required by the court and reported this to relevant authorities, the lake level was suddenly and quietly lowered quite noticeably. I was touring the Klamath Basin over the days when these events took place. Discovery of the excess water - water that could have been available to them for some time, had they known - was very exciting and certainly quite thought-provoking news to the farmers.

These events were rather quickly followed by Interior Secretary Norton's announcement that a small water release would be made to the farmers. Just how much excess water would have been available to the farmers and wildlife refuge, and how long the storage lake contained it, is perhaps known only to the relevant PacifiCorp personnel. Some might wonder if a potential conflict of interest could be involved since PacifiCorp stood to make more money by sending the water over its hydropower dams than by its release it to the farmers.

At this point, some earlier statements made by PCFFA's Glen Spain become rather interesting. He is quoted in a news report by Jude Noland titled *Feds Sued Over Fish Flows*. Spain was speaking about a suit that PCFFA filed in 2000 to force three federal agencies to comply with flow standards in a NMFS' 1995 biological opinion that was soon to become outdated, for operating dams in the federal Columbia River Power System. Noland's piece reveals Spain's explanation of the real purpose of PCFFA's lawsuit:

"'This is the shoe that everyone was hoping no one would drop,' said Glen Spain of the Pacific Coast Federation of Fisheries Associations, one of seven plaintiffs in the complaint. Others include Trout Unlimited, WaterWatch of Oregon, the NW Environmental Defense Center, Institute for Fisheries Resources, Oregon Natural Resources Council and the Sierra Club." That combination of organizational names should be pretty familiar by now.

Noland added: "Spain also said the real purpose of the complaint is to force the state of Idaho to choose between breaching the lower Snake River dams and releasing another million acre-feet of water now used by irrigators in the state. 'This makes people choose: either we do flow augmentation or we breach the dams,' he said. 'The dams cannot comply with flow standards unless you take more water from Idaho.'"

Thus, back in 2000 PCFFA admittedly sought to force government and the public to choose between hydropower or agricultural irrigation. Abundant electricity for the urban masses versus domestic food production. One or the other, electricity or water for farms. This doesn't sound like an organization that is terribly concerned with feeding people.

By 2000 the big environmental coalitions' push for dam breaching was roundly rejected by business, political and public outcry from various quarters defending hydropower as in the public's best interest. Interests like Direct Services Industries, a group of heavy industrial power users, and Columbia River Alliance, a coalition of power producers, industrial and other power users, represented by attorney-author James Buchal (*The Great Salmon Hoax*), worked in high gear at fighting breaching of the dams.

We should note that at least one of the Klamath Basin area's hydro dams is believed to block 90% of fish passage. Equally important to note is that some very prominent hydropower supporters tend to blame treaty fishing rights, and the tribes' rights to take part in fisheries management, for increasing the cost of hydropower operations. That particular battle, with its objections to Indian tribes' role in fisheries management and harvest practices, has been raging for years. Arguments put forth asserting that circumventing or overriding tribal fisheries management will keep hydropower costs down and enhance salmon recovery seem to intersect curiously with wild salmon proponents' objections to tribal interests.

Yet by the summer of 2001 when PCFFA and coalition's ESA fish suit produced the water shut-off to Klamath Basin farms, the entire general public was whipped into a veritable frenzy, a publicly shared panic and anger about possible power shortages. Everyone was up in arms about the specter of skyrocketing power bills. Even upwardly mobile urban and suburban dwellers who favor most environmental campaigns were worried about their own electrical supply.

It was the pre-September-11, pre-Enron-scandal summer of electrical brown-out jitters. Power pricing and purchase went crazy. The country was in a panic, demanding to know who was responsible for jeopardizing the juice much of it runs on. The country wanted more power, not less. Hydropower was in demand. Blame for loss of fish habitat focused away from hydropower and on situations like the Klamath Basin's farm irrigation project.

Government and the public had apparently made the choice that Spain's PCFFA said its coalition was trying to force, a choice between hydropower and water for farms. Fish versus farms in the Klamath Basin may really have also been about urban and industrial electricity versus farms, or power profits versus farms, for that matter.

One must wonder how much environmental coalitions like those suing in the Klamath Basin are influenced by such huge sums of money as those PacifiCorp contributed to the Nature Conservancy to buy 5,000 - 6,000 prime acres in the upper Klamath Basin, and vast acreage in various other locations around the world. Supposed high dollar mitigation schemes appear to be quite popular with international economic entities, transnational corporations and the mainstream environmental industry. They are not the sort of thing that small rural communities can afford.

It is interesting to note that The Nature Conservancy's basin lands were not denied irrigation water during the 2001 shut-off. TNC wasn't the only big environmental real estate buyer in the basin that summer. American Lands Conservancy, too, had already moved there, right into a downtown Klamath Falls office, actively pursuing purchase of the enviro-economically embattled farmers' lands.

CellTech is an algae harvesting and marketing industry operating on the Klamath Project's water storage lake. If the algae problem that is so fatal to ESA listed sucker fish is completely eradicated, how might CellTech's algae industry be affected? CellTech has apparently been profiting enough in the past to afford a hefty contribution, in addition to PacifiCorp's, to The Nature Conservancy's substantial land acquisition in the upper Klamath Basin.

What many call the Klamath Basin Crisis, is a tangle of court decisions, big government, big business and well-funded environmental players, and small community stakeholders just struggling to survive. The future of these small communities is being profoundly shaped by outside forces. The inhabitants of the rural landscape, in general, are facing very complicated, challenging times.

How will small natural resource communities fare in the courts in the future? Will Public Trust Doctrine ultimately favor or destroy the socioeconomic security of rural communities? Shouldn't the survival and self-determination of land-based communities be a public interest issue, too?

In light of those questions, it would be instructive, and, frankly, rather alarming, to look at two wild salmon papers underwritten by the Bullitt Foundation and prepared by Daniel Jack Chasen in 1998 and 2000. The Chasen papers propose to totally redefine the significance, value, stakeholders and management of salmon, and make wild salmon a public trust doctrine issue.

One reason these papers are significant is the underwriter. The Bullitt Foundation is one of the most wealthy, powerful and influential EGA environmental grantmakers operating in the Pacific Northwest. It, like all wealthy grantmaking foundations, chooses to fund those individuals and organizations which will carry out the objectives it approves. On Sunday, March 19, 2000, the Bullitt controlled *Seattle Post-Intelligencer* published a salmon special by Chasen.

Chasen's wild salmon papers generally focus on Puget Sound. However, they are significant to all natural resource-based rural communities because the objectives discussed therein have been adopted as the campaign goals of the environmental groups that form wild fish coalitions operating throughout the Northwest and the rest of the country. Both papers, we are told, were reviewed by a panel of experts. They exemplify the attitudes of most environmental organizations toward rural non-Indian and tribal values and sovereignty.

In his 2000 paper titled *The Rusted Shield: government's failure to enforce—or obey—our system of environmental law threatens the recovery of Puget Sound's wild salmon*, Chasen said: "Wild salmon are not in trouble because individual government officials, past or present, have ignored the law or bent it to serve the interests of favored constituents. They are in trouble because those individuals fit into a pattern…."

The title clearly says that government's failure to enforce or obey the law threatens salmon recovery. Yet the text says "salmon are not in trouble because individual government officials….have ignored the law or bent it". At the very outset of his argument, Chasen gives the reader cause to wonder about his capacity for logic and consistency. He goes on:

"Getting rid of a few rogue officials would be easy. Changing an historical pattern—changing a part of regional culture—will be hard. And yet, if we do not change it, there is little point in pretending to save the fish." Even though Chasen apparently has trouble knowing whether he believes government failure to enforce or obey the law is threatening salmon recovery or not, he nevertheless, is certain that "a part of regional culture" must be changed. Insisting that somebody's culture must be changed is a very serious statement, not to be taken lightly.

This is the kind of thought process and language so dominant in the environmental industry that human rights advocates need to start paying attention to. Who's culture is to be changed here? How? Why? Does this change promote self-determination and human dignity? Who has the right to demand this change?

Another gem of perverse, contradictory environmental industry wisdom: "Officials should not be indifferent to the risk of, for example, forcing farmers out of business. If western Washington farms disappear, they will probably not be replaced by anything more environmentally benign. But executive agencies have no authority to ignore the law." So farmers should be forced out of business, with prior knowledge that nothing *more* "environmentally benign" will replace them? This would sound absolutely insane to every third world citizen on earth, and should sound insane to everybody else, as well.

Chasen laments, "William Rodgers argues that the state's hydraulics code....could give the state control over virtually all activities that disrupt salmon habitat— but virtually no one takes an expansive view of the law's potential." Interestingly enough, on January 10, 2001, Public Employees for Environmental Responsibility (PEER), Pacific Coast Federation of Fishermen's Association (PCFFA), Institute for Fisheries Resources and Washington Trout filed a petition versus the Washington State Fish and Wildlife Commission and the Director of the Washington State Department of Fish and Wildlife. The purpose of the petition?

"Emergency petition to fully and effectively administer and enforce the hydraulic code and ensure that it prevents - rather than contributes to - a net loss of fisheries habitats and associated resources." Apparently this coalition decided to take Rodger's "expansive view of the law's potential", thus answering Chasen's lament. Unlikely coincidence.

A news release by Bill Bakke, touting Chasen's newly released paper, titled *New Report Says WA State Has Failed to Enforce Environmental Laws* quotes Emory Bundy, director of the Bullitt Foundation, on Chasen's *Rusted Shield.* "Because there isn't an adequate appreciation for the lack of enforcement of environmental laws, the Bullitt Foundation decided to do something about it," says the director of the foundation that supported Chasan's study.

Bundy said that Bullitt did not have "a strategy to make this a political agenda item yet". However, he added, "It is clear that unless we have public outrage we will get nowhere. However, I believe the Chasan report is the basis for major change in Washington." Certainly a foundation connected to major news media interests is capable of nurturing that public outrage. Bundy's remarks are a fair indication, one might reasonably surmise, that Bullitt money will play a role in promoting Chasen's recommendations. Bullitt doesn't just fund papers likes Chasen's, it funds environmental organizations, campaigns and lawsuits.

Wild Salmon for the Next Millennium: We Can Get There from Here, was written in 1998. It presents the wild salmon proponent's arguments and recommends certain actions. Chasen begins by telling his readers that salmon are in trouble, and that trouble is habitat, harvest and hatcheries. Thus, in one sweep he points the finger at farmers, loggers, fishermen and tribes.

Chasen says that the "jumble of overlapping and competing jurisdictions is itself a major problem....No one is in charge. Or everyone is. Either way, no single political entity has complete control over the harvest, much less over both harvest and habitat....The tribes have been a late but very significant addition to this jurisdictional stew."

He goes on to say, "The Boldt decision gave the treaty tribes a huge stake in the commercial fishery and forced the state to negotiate with them as equals." He also adds, "It did not relieve—it actually increased—the pressure on managers to let the fishing fleet catch every last fish....And it did nothing to halt the destruction of habitat." So there you have the wild salmon activist's attitude toward the tribes.

Chasen further says that the hatcheries, which produce such ample runs and feed so many people, "represent society's best effort to have its cake and eat it, too." He maintains that hatcheries harm wild salmon and "put pressure on fishery managers to let fishers deplete wild salmon runs." All hatchery science arguments aside, his solutions still represent a threat to tribal values, welfare and sovereignty, as well as that of other fishing and land-based communities.

The section called "Stop The Harvest", says: "The survival and recovery of wild stocks must become the primary goal....the state must forbid any commercial fishing on mixed stocks that include wild runs....Tribal fisheries must let wild salmon escape, too. The tribes have a vested interest in protecting salmon and salmon habitat, but not necessarily in protecting wild, as opposed to hatchery, fish. And yet, no management scheme can succeed unless the tribes cooperate."

There's the rub for the tribes. The environmental industry sees them as useful for protecting salmon habitat, but not the lauded "wild" salmon. Instead, they see the tribes' sovereignty and fishing rights as an obstacle. The Native Fish Society, based in Oregon, posts Chasen's work on their extensive wild fish web site. The Society's April - March 2000 Program Report speaks even more bluntly—

"Assuming that all populations are subject to Co-management means that the state and the tribes must negotiate conservation policy on all populations of salmon and steelhead. As we saw in the last legislature, the tribes tried to remove the application of the Oregon Wild Fish Policy on all salmon and steelhead populations in Oregon above Bonneville Dam. If they had succeeded in this legislative effort, the tribes would have reserved for themselves the right to manage all salmon and steelhead in Oregon above Bonneville Dam."

It goes on: "This means all standards and criteria the state had adopted to protect native, wild salmonids would be deleted. The tribes characterized this effort as a spiritual and cultural necessity which played well among legislators on both sides of the aisle. In reality, however, the tribes wanted to defeat the Wild Fish Policy so they could operate hatchery programs free of any conservation constraint to protect wild, native populations, most of which are ESA-listed species."

One wonders why the tribes might be leery of wild salmon policy? Well, Chasen says the fishing prohibitions should last at least for the length of a wild run's natural cycle, up to seven years, that we "must be willing to sacrifice some current interests", get rid of hatcheries, circumvent tribal management and scrap the concept of maximum sustainable yield.

Some of the tribes' dependable fisheries that support families and feed people are some of those "current interests" that Chasen et al say must be sacrificed. The Native Fish Society's sniping about tribal spiritual and cultural necessity 'playing well' among legislators is particularly illuminating. The racial overtones are apparent. There are a lot of people not being fed salmon inferred in all these words, and a lot of those people will be Indian.

Chasen explains: "The focus must shift from the welfare of fishers—the 'yield'—to the welfare of fish." He says that "harvest managers must spread fishing *opportunities* among the largest number of people....salmon as a commodity can't compete with salmon as a recreational resource...salmon caught by a sport fisher puts more money into the state economy than a salmon caught in a gillnet. The economic impact of sport fishing should be measured not in fish *per se* but in fishing days."

Again, these words about the superior economic value of sport fishing don't promise to feed many people. Most profoundly, Chasen explains: "The activity, rather than the meat, provides most of the value." This notion flies in the face of the tribes, commercial fishers, and the value of human life in general. He claims that to those who "value" the regional commercial fishing tradition, the "opportunity" to fish is more important than the size of the catch. It is more than difficult to imagine any commercial fisherman who supports a family agreeing with this absurd statement.

Ironically, a recent Middle Atlantic edition of the Fisherman recently reported: "Right now, extremist environmental groups are waging a subtle battle in California and other states for the public's premier coastal recreational areas. Within the past year, schemes have been hatched that would shut down more than 60 percent of Southern California's best sport fishing grounds....Already, 'No Fishing' proposals have circulated throughout New England, Florida and other parts of the Southeast. It's just a matter of time before these well-organized and richly financed groups tell you that you're no longer welcome in your public waters." The wild fish crowd have no problem using sport fishermen, then sinking the knife into their backs, too.

Astoundingly, Chasen goes on to rationalize that if commercial fishermen only catch a few salmon, they're not really commercial fishermen. He supports this ridiculous statement by saying that no non-Indian fisherman makes a living fishing Puget Sound salmon anymore anyway. One callous absurdity just leads to another. Apparently the fact that some Indian fishermen still do make a living in the Sound doesn't matter. They all count for naught in the "wild" salmon ethos.

Quite highhandedly Chasen then says the opportunity to be a commercial fisherman "may" be passed on *if wild runs recover*. Yet
immediately thereafter, he also says, *"But enabling commercial
fishers to catch large numbers of fish is not a realistic management goal."* How nonchalant he is in asserting the elite wild
salmon ethos. Apparently, in this wild salmon environmental industry milieu, there *is* no effort planned to feed a large number of
people with free running domestic salmon at *any* time in the future.

Under a section titled "Close The Hatcheries" Chasen tells us
that we must stop raising salmon that will mingle with wild fish,
halt mixed-stock fisheries and stop using wild fish stocks for eggs.
This eliminates an awful lot of food now and in the future. Then
he says, *"The tribes must be offered inducement to do the same.
If they refuse, the federal government must force them to cooperate."*

The public should take notice when words like "inducement" and
"force" are used in the same breath, particularly the Indian public.
This statement alone should cause the tribes great concern. There
are extremely powerful, wealthy people funding the implementa-
tion of these objectives.

In this ethos where a scientifically questionable notion of salmon
wildness takes precedence over feeding people, hatcheries should
only be used to rescue wild fish on the brink of extinction or "to
produce fish in places where no wild populations exist." Chasen
says any hatcheries that are allowed should be "independently
monitored". Obviously, neither government nor tribe are up to the
task in Chasen's estimation. Yet he insists that tribes should be
forced to cooperate in this usurpation of their sovereignty and
treaty rights if they resist.

The paper recommends that the taxpaying public be told that hatcheries have failed and made the problem worse. Chasen says that
we should bring fish into population centers, but this tactic "should
not be confused with saving wild salmon". He explains: "In terms
of salmon per dollar spent, it wouldn't be cost-effective. *But* producing the largest number of salmon per dollar shouldn't be the

goal...", rather restoring "some" urban streams "would have several virtues"—

"It would increase the value of salmon as a regional amenity....pay political dividends....give urban voters who don't fish a concrete stake in salmon recovery." Other than this blatant political PR strategy, Chasen says we should:

"Instead of trying to reengineer small stretches of degraded stream, create linkages that will enable salmon to use habitat that is already of high quality or already is protected.... Expand protected areas. Except where there will be specific aesthetic, recreational or educational benefits—or where it is possible to connect large areas of relatively intact habitat—don't invest public money in habitat that has already been badly degraded."

Think about those recommendations for a moment. Essentially, Chasen is saying that a few urban streams should be cleaned up for salmon so that city dwellers acquire an attitude that having wild salmon around is an amenity to which they are entitled, and will vote and otherwise act to insist on their perceived right to this amenity. Other than that "political dividend", he recommends we forget cleaning up the worst streams and focus on "preserving" and "protecting" what boils down to all the rural areas.

In reality, that translates into rural job and property losses, continued degraded waters in populated areas, and the same old pattern of using rural communities as mitigation areas for continued urban excesses. It is highly suggestive of magnifying the current state of mob rule over the rural minority. Chasen recommends that once these sorts of regional priorities are established, temporary citizen's committees should be created on an ad hoc basis to draw up habitat plans for the watersheds where they live. This process is essentially already going on in Washington state among various citizen's watershed management planning efforts under government auspices.

Chasen says we must stop "subsidizing" projects that destroy salmon habitat—"Society has, for example, pumped many millions of dollars into projects that protect pastures or scattered houses from occasional floods." And, of course, he says we must eliminate what he considers "subsidized" logging in "public" forests. The fact that he is constantly talking about rearranging and recreating rural America does not really seem to give him, nor the entire wild salmon milieu, a moment's pause doubting their right to carry such plans out. And why should it? It is not their culture they plan to destroy. The trained ear can hear echoes of manifest destiny in their plans.

A section titled "Take Fishery Management Beyond Politics" makes the wild salmon proponent's objectives profoundly clear. Chasen asserts that we must find ways to override the existing salmon management institutions. He says that they have not protected "the broader public interest", and "[s]omeone must be able to control harvest policies both inside and outside the state." Obviously, that means controlling the fishing tribes, as well.

His solution?…"get a special master appointed by a federal district court to oversee all harvest regulations." Chasen states in no uncertain terms: "The current task is therefore to identify the issues and do the legal research for a civil suit that will lead to appointment of a special master." This tactic, in reality, is nothing less than a blatant legal assault strategy on tribal sovereignty and self-determination. At this point, recall that the Bullitt Foundation already contributes substantial sums to environmental lawsuits, along with many other fabulously wealthy grantmakers.

Make Wild Salmon A Public Trust is the section that presents the most broad-based threat to the survival of rural land-based communities. Chasen stoutly recommends, "Develop and bring a case that establishes the principal that spawning streams are protected by the public trust doctrine." He explains that this will protect "the people's common heritage"; it is for the benefit of the public; that thus extending the public trust doctrine will provide "a new legal tool" and…"It will also help develop a rationale for treating habitat, as well as fish, as everybody's resource." The Action Plan reiterates: "Expand the legal possibilities. Develop and bring a case that establishes the principal that spawning streams are protected by the public trust doctrine."

Chasen's paper also recommends that we 'give the Growth Management Act more teeth and a larger brain' - the same GMA that decimates already staggering remote rural economies. And, since "[r]egulation is necessary but not sufficient", he asserts that we should "[b]uy riparian land, development rights and conservation easements. Unlike regulation, this would be permanent....and would not make the regulated citizens, who are mostly rural, resent the urban majority that expects them to atone for society's historic sins. It also would signal a deeper public commitment: in this culture, if we really want something, we should be willing to pay for it."

Those remarks clearly reflect how out-of-touch and unconcerned with rural communities Chasen's ilk really are. Government and environmental industry land acquisition "willing seller" schemes have been the bane of rural people's continued socioeconomic existence for decades. The "willing seller" myth is just as much a myth in today's non-Indian rural America as it was, and still is, in 17th - 21st Century Indian America. That the politically dominant urbanites "should" be willing to pay for it is no comfort whatsoever.

Chasen then recommends that the environmental industry 'sell wild salmon to the region like Paul Allen sold a new football stadium' by developing and running "a public relations campaign that will use public service spots, bus signs, direct mail and other devices to emphasize salmon as....a resource that belongs to everyone". He says we must "redefine the significance of salmon...broaden the definition of stakeholders...treat wild salmon as everyone's resource". We've all seen the resultant flood of slick TV campaign advertisements.

Chasen maintains that "[w]e can't keep putting fishermen first....the traditional user groups should not be allowed to call the shots....they should not be in a position to reap the most benefits....people at large shouldn't pay to restore salmon for their sake....Salmon must no longer be treated as a commodity."

So there you have it, fishermen, tribes and all you eaters of fish. The environmental elite decree that salmon must no longer be treated as food.

Then Chasen makes a suggestion that is certainly quite contrary to our representative democracy: "A coalition of nonprofit groups could sponsor a 'people's jury' that could deliver a verdict on the state's recovery plan before it went to NMFS. This would draw widespread attention both to the issues and to the idea that a dozen ordinary citizens can decide where the public interest really lies."

A dozen "ordinary" citizens - members of so-called non-profit environmental industry groups - can decide where the public interest lies? I think not. We still have minds of our own and the ballot box.

The Bullitt funded paper reiterates in its final action plan section: "….a lot of fish are caught outside the state's jurisdiction. Therefore, a non-profit group or groups must identify the issues and do the legal research for a civil suit that will lead to appointment of a special master….Build a constituency for wild fish. Develop and run a public relations campaign that redefines the significance of salmon….Expand the legal possibilities. Develop and bring a case that establishes the principal that spawning streams are protected by the public trust doctrine".

So there you have it, farmers, ranchers, orchardists, loggers, fishermen, tribes and all you eaters of fish. Cowboy, Indian and fisherman alike, circle the wagons and fishing boats. The environmental conflict industry has plans to turn fish and public trust against all of you. It is too much like manifest destiny to be ignored.

On May 26, 2002, Great Falls Tribune reports: "*Environmental groups awarded attorney fees* ….Two environmental groups were awarded more than $200,000 in attorney fees stemming from a dispute with the U.S. Forest Service over plans to cut timber burned during forest fires….U.S. District Judge Donald Molloy ordered the agency to pay about $124,000 to the Wilderness Society and about $76,000 to the Friends of the Bitterroot….Spike Thompson, acting forest supervisor, said money will be taken from restoration activities to pay the groups."

Isn't that a bit ironic? No, perverse, really. The environmental industry's attorney costs are initially funded by unbelievably wealthy foundations, then they are reimbursed for these fees out of environmental restoration funds. That's certainly not going to help imperiled fish and wildlife. This is the environmental industry at work, pitting public trust against Indian, fisherman, logger and farmer alike.

-Chapter Nine-

Cowboys, Indians and Indian Cowboys

The whole country has heard stories about the "sagebrush rebellion" in the West, mostly in terms derogatory to the livestock rancher. For many years there has been good reason for the conflict between Western family ranch communities - struggling to survive in today's increasingly globalized economy - and the wealthy environmental industry and federal land management agencies that control the family ranch's prospects for survival.

In April 2002, the environmental industry stepped up its campaign to remove family ranches from the rural landscape with an ambitious proposal to "buy out" 25,000 federal lands livestock grazing leases. What the public is not told, is that without the range provided by those grazing leases, Western family ranching and the rural communities it supports cannot survive.

The environmental industry ignores the fact that these US ranching families are small producers of high quality, healthy, domestic free range beef, as though it is irrelevant to public health and domestic self-sufficiency. Those who would cleanse the rural landscape of family ranching communities neglect to mention that only big industry - large feedlot producers, wealthy owners of vast tracts of private land, and foreign producers - can continue to operate in this kind of enviro-economic climate.

Yet the National Public Lands Grazing Campaign mailed its buyout proposal to nearly 26,000 livestock grazing permittees across the West in April 2002. The campaign proposes what sounds like tempting big money under a plan that currently is illegal. The

172

Western Watersheds Project, American Lands Alliance, Center for Biological Diversity, Committee for Idaho's High Desert, Forest Guardians and Oregon Natural Desert Association have joined forces to promote the campaign.

Congressional action is necessary to make the coalition's proposal legal and to provide funding. However, the campaign has attracted the usual broad support from well-funded environmental industry groups with 85 organizations endorsing the plan, according to the campaign's April 10 news release. Even more disturbing, it is being taken seriously by politicians.

Western Watersheds' public information officer in Hailey, Idaho, Keith Raether, claims the proposal letters are getting responses. The April 10 campaign news release quotes an unidentified Idaho cattleman endorsing the plan, claiming he would only speak anonymously. One can only wonder if the alleged rancher is someone like Ted Turner, the wealthy sort that doesn't need federal grazing permits. The anti-grazing campaign maligns livestock grazing with claims that it has degraded "about 80 percent of all streams and riparian ecosystems in the arid West" and "175 plant and animal species, from sage grouse to grizzly bears, are threatened or endangered, all or in part, by grazing on federal rangelands."

Yet Wayne Burleson, a pasture management consultant working out of Absarokee, paints the factual picture in his guest opinion for the Billings Gazette on April 19. "I know for fact that simply removing the American grazing animal from Western native range land will not fix land health problems. Just the opposite will happen; this action, long-term, will ruin the land. If all this livestock grazing is removed from the dry western range land, the land will look better for a short period of time (heal overgrazed spots) but will ultimately end up being much worse than before." The range expert explains that long-term non-disturbance of the land results in plant stagnation that chokes out certain biological cycles. The plants then begin to die, as observed, he says, on Montana's long-term Conservation Reserve Program land.

Even more alarming, Burleson says removal of livestock grazers from the rural Western landscape will harm both human and wildlife communities. "If this group of folks accomplish these 'buy-outs' you will see an increase in failed rural economies and fewer jobs in rural communities, poor quality vegetation, increasing fire danger, decreasing wildlife over the long-term, along with a grass stagnation and a rise in brush and trees. If these are the goals, then stopping livestock grazing should be considered. However, I assume that healthier land and happy people is the better goal."

Burleson warns, "….we better take a long-term look and see what rest [of the land] will result in before we make decisions to stop public land grazing. We can fix land problems with range land management. You don't fix land problems by not managing the land."

But healthier land and happy people ceased to be environmentalism's goal way back when it sold out to big money politics. The anti-grazing proposal's campaign director is the infamous Andy Kerr. He was also a leader of the notorious spotted-owl campaign that shut down small timber businesses, putting thousands out of work, causing egregious socioeconomic damage across the rural West. Astoundingly, Kerr claims that the federal government encourages citizens to sue. "The stick approach is important," he then intones, "but environmentalists also want the government to implement the carrot approach." So, in Kerr's buy-out plan announcement, ranchers are told the onerous proposal could "save them from tough economic times, a losing occupation and a vanishing way of life".

Those are pretty harsh words— "a losing occupation". Kerr and the campaign he directs obviously mean to take advantage of those "tough economic times" to make this "vanishing way of life" vanish quite swiftly. Kerr has the gall to proclaim: "Federal grazing permit buyouts are ecologically imperative, economically rational, fiscally prudent, socially compassionate and politically pragmatic. It's a win-win-win for permittees, taxpayers and the environment."

The anti-grazing proposal is not a win for family agriculture, wildlife, the land, or the general public. It is certainly not compassionate toward the ranch families and communities it will destroy. It is, however, surely politically pragmatic for Kerr and his kind. This is the rather chilling elitist attitude that family ranch communities have had to contend with for many years. Many see it as essentially a continuation of the old Northern industrial elite's hegemony over the rural West.

Few people in the American mainstream that have heard about the "sagebrush rebellion", however, realize that these very same conflicts and pressures extend to Indian ranching communities. Nor does the American mainstream realize what the "cowboy life" has come to mean for many Western tribal communities and Indian families.

The Senate Committee on Indian Affairs Februrary 16, 1999 "Indian Agriculture" report describes the important role of agriculture for tribal communities. "Agriculture has been a part of the Native American way of life throughout history….In modern times, Native Americans use their lands and natural resources to provide staples and other foods for consumption as well as to improve their economic self-sufficiency, agriculture income and reservation employment….the agricultural sector constitutes the second largest revenue generator and employer to Indian country. According to the U.S. Census, some 70 percent of Indian agriculture production comes from livestock operations."

Clearly, the fate of Indian agriculture, particularly ranching, is highly important to the socioeconomic welfare of many Western indigenous communities.

The report prepared for the Senate committee by the Intertribal Agriculture Council also includes forestry as agriculture. "54.4 million acres of Indian homelands remaining in the contiguous United States today contain nearly 47 million acres of agricultural lands used for the production of crops, livestock, or both. In 1984, agricultural products grown on Indian lands were valued at $548.6 million. As a comparison, commercial forests occupy 5.8 million acres of Indian lands and generate stumpage values of $61.5 million, and mineral income totals $230.7 million from all sources; including oil, gas, coal, and minerals." The report goes on to discuss current challenges to Indian agriculture as a whole.

The general public is also widely unaware of the long struggle Indian America put forth, since the reservations were first established, to participate in the US agricultural economy and the self-determination and socioeconomic benefits that agricultural life would bring. Yet ever since the reservations were established, agriculture is what both government and social commentators lauded as the best prospect for Indian self-sufficiency. Detailed studies have been done on those years that illuminate the obstacles tribes working to pursue farming and ranching faced right from the outset, through the allotment, assimilation and termination policy years.

Among those that can be recommended to gain an understanding of tribal struggles to participate in the agricultural economy are *The Cheyenne and Arapaho Ordeal* by Donald J. Berthrong, *An Unspeakable Sadness* by David J. Wishart and *When Indians Became Cowboys* by Peter Iverson. These studies will also explain why many remote reservation communities remain pockets of crushing poverty to this day.

Wishart explains: "One of the problems was that there existed an inherent contradiction in federal policy: the civilization program was never given the necessary funds to ever have a chance....The main funding for the program throughout the nineteenth century came from the Indians' own money, which they received for the sale of their lands. However, Congress was always niggardly in funding the Indian Office. Requested appropriations were invariably cut by congressmen who, reflecting their constituents' views, regarded any payments to the Indians—even payments owed for the sale of Indian lands—as a form of welfare. Always short of funds and constantly pressured to facilitate frontier expansion, the Indian Office obtained cessions at the lowest cost possible, then used the payments to try to make the Indians self-sufficient so that they would not need support in the future. The result was that the Indians' land base rapidly diminished, but the civilization program stalled for want of funds."

Berthrong provides further insight: "Members of Congress were nearly unanimous in their insistence that only minimal expenditures be made in behalf of the Indian people. Appropriations exceeding those specified in treaties or agreements were bitterly denounced on the floor of Congress as extravagant and needless waste of revenue. Classed as gratuities, nontreaty funds designated to educate and to provide food, medicine, farming implements, stock animals, clothing, or vocational instruction to Indians were rigorously examined by congressional committees in unceasing efforts to appropriate only the smallest subventions possible. Rarely in the last quarter of the nineteenth or early twentieth century did Congress provide the funds needed...."

Iverson goes right to the heart of the matter— "Americans prided themselves on being people of laws, of the sanctity of contracts, of the importance of keeping one's word. Somehow, the treaties fell outside of this framework. Agreements with individual tribes did not have to be honored. As they have in previous generations, non-Indians muttered that the Native peoples did not deserve the lands they claimed. Unfortunately for the Indians, officials within the federal government agreed."

More than just the attitudes in Congress and the federal bureaucracy frustrated the tribes attempts to enter the agricultural economy and achieve economic self-sufficiency. They also had to contend with continual land loss and theft of farming equipment. Range encroachment resulted in starvation of their cattle and destruction of their fields.

Vine Deloria Jr. recounts the bitter experience of the Oglala's participation in the cattle business. "The people had developed large herds of cattle by 1916, and were fairly prosperous. They had extensive pony herds, and raised some of the finest horses in the Northern Plains....In 1917, under a new government policy, the agent for the Oglalas sold their cattle, allegedly for the war needs, and leased their lands out to white cattlemen who were bringing cattle up from the South to graze....The cattle market broke following the war, making it impossible for the Oglalas to reenter the cattle business...."

The Eastern tribes had been accomplished agricultural peoples long before the colonists arrived, and as such had the experience necessary to begin anew albeit on far less suitable land than their

original homelands. Indeed, Indian America has a rich agricultural tradition which gave the world hundreds of varieties corn,
beans and squash, only to name a few, in addition to a vast body of
medicinal plant knowledge. Who can forget that the pilgrims would
not even have survived their first year if the Wampanoag had not
taught them how to farm in America?

Yet even with their expertise at farming, the transition from freedom to participating in the US agricultural economy on their reservations was fraught with obstacles for the Eastern tribes. Many
an Eastern tribe experienced resettlement due to a treaty, only to
find their productive, newly developed farmlands coveted, followed
by yet another removal.

The interior Western tribes, however, lived a more wide-ranging
life as they followed the seasons than was necessary in the East,
gathering and hunting for subsistence rather than farming and hunting. Making matters even more difficult for them, the government often insisted that Western tribes become crop farmers when
their land was really far more suited to livestock grazing. As
Iverson notes, "Washington did more to hinder than to help the
evolution of Indian cattle ranching." It should not be difficult to
understand that these bitter experiences sometimes linger in the
background of today's rural landscape.

Yet the tribes persisted over the decades, and today, as the Senate
committee report reflects, ranching provides the means for many
tribal communities throughout the West for a self-sufficient, realistic life on the land. It is just as LaDuke pointed out to the EGA
regarding the Western Shoshone Dann sisters in 1992—livestock
ranching gives Indian people a realistic, self-sufficient life on the
land. This is an outdoor life, as Iverson and others have remarked,
that involves direct contact with the land and the seasons, a life
that allowed Indians to remain Indian.

This ranching life that tribes and individual Indian families fought
so hard to enter and to succeed in will hardly now be given up
without a fight. Over the last several generations Indian ranching
has become a vital part of Western tribal community stability. The
National Congress of American Indians' current president, Tex

Hall, for instance, comes from a generational ranching family.

In recent years, as non-Indian ranching has come under pressure from the global market, the environmental industry and federal land management agencies, so too has Indian ranching. As Iverson points out, where the two communities had to varying degrees been at odds in the old days, today Indian and non-Indian ranchers face the same challenges and the same enemies.

Iverson suggests that ever since the 1960's, both Indian and non-Indian ranchers face the very same threat that confronted Indians in the nineteenth century— both are now surrounded by a society that does not understand them and has very different ideas about how they should use the land. He observes that Indian and non-Indian cowboys share both a common sense of place and tradition, and an uncertain future.

That future is uncertain because some very powerful outside interests think they have a higher purpose for the land than today's Indian and non-Indian agricultural peoples, that same old echo of manifest destiny thinking. It is on the rugged terrain of the American West that we see the first signs of Indian and non-Indian communities facing those threats together. Both the state of Idaho and the Kalispel Tribe, for instance, sued the federal government over the Clinton administration's "roadless plan" that cut off virtually all local access and use of vast areas of Western forests. The story of non-Indian Nevada ranchers and Western Shoshone livestock grazers is one that perplexes those unfamiliar with the realities of the rural Western landscape.

Both non-Indian rural Nevada and Western Shoshone grazers have been at odds with punitive environmental regulation and federal management agencies for the last two decades. The US Forest Service, the US Fish and Wildlife Service and the federal Bureau of Land Management have been making life more and more difficult for rural Nevada ranching communities. Similar difficulties are experienced in terms of logging for both Indian and non-Indian rural communities throughout the West.

In the spring of 2002, in Elko County and the Te-Moak Western

Shoshone reservation, the history of a broken treaty and modern
day oppressive federal land management result in news headlines
that are rather surprising and thought-provoking to those who are
outsiders to rural Western life. There, both red and white cowboys, so to speak, participate in the same protests, objecting to the
same government agency oppression.

Two years earlier, on the Colville Reservation in Washington state,
environmentalist sentiment and influence against cattle grazing had
reached the point that the tribal council of the Colville Confederated Tribes decided to put the whole matter before a tribal membership advisory vote in March of 2000.

Before the tribal membership were three proposals made by the
tribal council's Natural Resources Committee that would have
drastically restricted cattle grazing on the reservation. The committee proposed to prohibit non-tribal members from leasing land
for cattle grazing and sharply increase range lease payments for
tribal member ranchers. The committee also proposed to make
the entire reservation closed range. However, the Colville Indian
ranchers were not about to accept these proposals without a fight.

Charlie Moses, tribal member, and board member and past president of the Colville Indian Livestock Association, spoke out in no
uncertain terms. "It appears to be an effort to eliminate grazing on
the reservation. If they take the non-Indian cattlemen off, we
think we're the next in line to go." The cattlemen took their opposition to the Spokane newspapers and TV media. Moses said the
livestock association strongly opposes all three of the Natural Resource Committee's proposals, including the "divisive" proposal
to ban non-Indian cattlemen. That position was unanimous, he
said, at a meeting of 100 to 150 livestock association members,
approximately two-thirds of whom are Colville tribal members.

Moses condemned the racially divisive nature of the proposals,
saying, "We have neighbors who have lived here probably 80 or
90 years now, and they've been good neighbors. Their kids and
ours go to school together. It's hard enough to have little kids
come up without being prejudiced without something like this to
start dividing people." In addition, Moses warned that the live-

stock association believes increasing tribal members' grazing fees and eliminating open range could force Indian ranchers out of business. There are approximately 50 - 60 Indian ranchers on the Colville reservation, and 20 - 30 non-member ranchers, many of whom are married to tribal members.

Tribal Councilwoman Doll Watt, a member of the Natural Resources Committee that made the proposals, said that "numerous tribal members" are concerned about damage to natural species habitat and water pollution from cattle grazing. Moses assured the public that the Colville reservation cattle ranchers are working hard to protect streams and lakes with fences to keep cattle out of any sensitive areas.

Yet Watt also claimed that fences themselves are a problem. That does sound like an indication that even closed range may not satisfy the people she was speaking of. "When they were growing up, they didn't have all these fences locking them out from their hunting regions. They weren't locked out from their huckleberry picking and their herbs and their medicines," Watt said.

However, Moses maintains cattle grazing does not have to be incompatible with concerns about the environment or retaining tribal culture. "With proper management, we can have all the good things and still run cattle. Grass is a renewable resource. It comes back every year." Similar arguments can be made, one should note, for the tribes' timber business.

Fences are necessary to keep livestock out of inappropriate grazing areas, whether ecologically sensitive areas or fields and gardens. Yet fences have gates or can at least be climbed over or under if they stand between you and a gathering or hunting area. They certainly do not flat out exclude the elderly or physically challenged like wilderness designations and remote access road closures promoted by the environmental industry do. There should surely be younger folks and family members in the community who will gladly assist any elderly who might have difficulty with fences. Speaking from the background of a farm kid, I never saw the auntie's have to go berry picking without plenty of extra hands anxious to help. It is reasonable to expect that the socioeconomic benefits successful participation in the agricultural economy has brought to the community and its children can be appreciated, and balanced with other cultural concerns.

Colville tribal member and non-member grazers have a total of about 3,500 cattle per group. That comes to a grand total of 7,000 head of cattle, which is merely half the number of cattle the Bureau of Indian Affairs determines is the capacity of the Colvilles' reservation range land. At 1.4 million acres, it is the second largest reservation in the US. Clearly the cattlemen on the Colville are not overgrazing. Moses said that Indian cattlemen usually run small herds of about 50 cows, and that a herd of 200 may be the largest run on the reservation. Since profit margins are already exceedingly thin, the Colville reservation ranchers could not afford higher grazing fees or the cost of all the additional fencing required by a change to closed range policies.

For those unacquainted with rural Western life, open range means there will be areas where livestock are able to wander across the remote rural roads. Rather than slowing down in these areas, as one really should do for wildlife anyway, some folks feel they should be able to speed along just as though they are still on city freeways. Despite the fact that far more people hit deer with their speeding vehicles, rarely ever hitting livestock, some people still feel they must complain about cows.

You do need to fence livestock out of your garden or yard if you live in an open range area, but you have to fence the deer out anyway. Deer are far more numerous and a lot harder to keep out, requiring expensive two tier hog wire, whereas stringing fence wire will do for cows. Cattle are very effective land management tools when used properly to prevent invasive non-native weed infestations and reduce brush that would otherwise be white hot fuel for wildfire.

When the Colville tribal membership's votes were counted, not only had the Colville Indian Livestock Association stood up for the reservation's Indian and non-Indian grazers alike, but so had the tribal membership. Colville Confederated Tribes' Chairwoman, Collene Cawston, announced the results. A large majority of the

474 enrolled members who voted in the advisory ballot rejected all three of the Natural Resource Committee's proposals. The Colville Business Council has the final yea or nay on these matters, but Colville tribal members made their decision quite clear, voting nearly two to one against the anti-grazing proposals. "No" on taking grazing permits away from non-tribal-members. "No" on taking all lands out of open range. "No" on raising the fees for grazing permits for tribal members.

Tribal members interviewed by the media who opposed the proposals expressed concerns about racial divisiveness, impact on Indian ranch families, tribal community relations, and concerns about a negative impact on tribal relations with the area's non-Indian residents. The Colville's enjoy the non-Indian community's patronage of a variety of tribal businesses. The tribes' economy and socioeconomic stability, as part of the area's whole economy, was clearly a concern, as well as what image the tribe would project to their neighbors.

This is the kind of well-considered thinking and resistance to divisiveness that land-based Indian and non-Indian communities will be needing more and more in order to survive what has become America's new war over land rights with federal encroachment and a jaded environmental industry. Both communities now face common threats to their rural way of life and socioeconomic stability.

The Associated Press reported on March 21, 2000: "Lester Herman, chairman of the Colville Indian Livestock Association, warned in debate prior to the vote against taking grazing permits from nonmembers. It would be seen as discrimination and cause some people to stop patronizing tribal casinos and houseboat rentals, he said....Kicking white ranchers off the range was the issue most opposed by cattlemen because it pitted member against nonmember on a reservation with many mixed marriages and whites who have lived on the reservation for generations, he said.... 'We're all after the same thing, and there's no need to fight about it,' agreed Nadene Naff, a cattlewoman and vocal opponent of the measures."

There were also unpublicized allegations made by tribal members that cited misconduct and intimidation by some grazing opponents intended to influence tribal members to vote for the proposals. A Colville tribal ranching acquaintance reported to me that some tribal members called for an FBI investigation of the allegations. There were complaints for years, I was told, of outside influence and interference from non-Indian environmental groups located off the reservation. Whether or not the requested investigation would occur was unclear. However, the tribal member's advisory vote had already made their outlook on the grazing issue clear.

The following year, the Colville Indian Livestock Association partnered with the Colville Reservation-Ferry County area Washington State University Cooperative Extension to publish and distribute factual information about ranching and the agricultural community on the reservation. *A Look At Past, Present and Future Faces of Agriculture On the Colville Reservation* educates the public about the history and value of the Colville's participation in the agricultural economy.

"By the time the Colville Indian Reservation was established in 1872, agriculture had firmly taken root. Indians were allotted 80 - 160 acres near creeks, lakes or close to springs (a water source and grazing land for cattle and horses were primary considerations in determining allotments). Tribal members built homes and planted large gardens." Those interested in farming, it says, were given a team of horses, farm implements, seed and experienced assistance.

"Chief Tonasket wintered a large herd of cattle in the Okanogan Valley, moving them to the San Poil in the summer. In 1884 he started summering them in the Curlew area. He mowed hay on the lush meadows of the San Poil and the south end of Curlew Lake. He knew that the cattle might need feed some winters, but for the most part they grazed in open land all winter. The winter of 1889-1890 was a livestock killer, called the great freeze. But thanks to the stockpile of mowed hay, Tonasket saved more of his cattle and horses than others." Not only was Tonasket a proven herdsmen, but practical about business matters as well. The publication mentions that Tonasket used to also run 1,000 head of sheep, but "didn't keep them as long as he made more money with cattle."

As mentioned earlier, tribal member Lucy Covington used proceeds from her cattle to finance her travels to Washington, DC, and all the activities that successfully fought termination of the Colville Reservation. This cattle-woman, at home on the ranch or in traditional ceremonial garb, the publication says, "will always be revered for the leadership and sacrifice shown in saving the Reservation." What better recommendation of the value of cattle ranching could anyone ask for than that?

The local livestock association's publication familiarized the reader with Colville tribal ranching families and range science past to present. It gives a sound, understandable presentation of range practices, improvement projects to protect natural species and ecosystem health, and the rarely publicized benefits agriculture brings to wildlife. That Indian food producers would have to go to such lengths to defend their livelihoods seems terribly ironic, but it is certainly a sign of the times and the threats family farms and ranches across America face.

One change of growing concern in the rural landscape that the urban voter and petition signer is certainly unaware of, is reflected in the May 9, 2002 *@griculture Online* news report, *NCBA pleased with farm bill's new Grassland Reserve Program.* "The Nature Conservancy and the National Cattlemen's Beef Association are hailing the creation of the Grassland Reserve Program (GRP)....The GRP, which was included in the 2002 Farm Bill that passed the Senate Wednesday afternoon, is a project the two groups have been working on together for about two years....Under the GRP, ranchers and other private grassland owners who enroll agree to place 10, 15, 20 or 30 -year rental contracts or 30 -year or permanent easements on their land....The farm bill authorizes up to 2 million acres to be enrolled in the program, at a cost of up to $254 million."

However, the brief news report did not explain to those unfamiliar with rural reality that such programs impact family ranch busi-

nesses - which all have far less land to spare for such so-called
conservation easements - much more negatively than big industry
beef producers, payment or no payment. Family livestock owners and family farms have witnessed an increased tendency over
the years of national organizations that once represented them
well to now favor the big producers.

National level partnerships with organizations like The Nature
Conservancy that have a reputation throughout rural America associated with controversial land grabs and outside big money interests, are not a good sign for family agricultural enterprises.
That this trend runs concurrent with a national campaign to eliminate livestock grazers from federal land should be very disturbing
to anyone concerned about the survival of family agriculture.

This trend, combined with the environmental industry's deep pockets to wage a continual national anti-grazing campaign, from lobbying to media to the courtroom, presents a persistent threat to
family livestock ranching communities. It is clear that smaller
local farming and livestock associations, communities and enterprises will have to support each other's needs more and more to
survive. They all face expanding regulatory pressures applied by
the environmental industry and federal agencies, economic globalization pressures, and the combined political forces affecting
agriculture today. Perhaps the urbanized majority's media-induced
misconception of the inhabitants of the rural landscape is the most
tragic of these perils.

The national campaign to eliminate cattle grazing on federal lands
has been persistently chugging along for a decade now, since the
"Cattle Free by '93" campaign, making incremental progress toward the goal that will eliminate the small family livestock producer from the American landscape. In today's money-driven
world of the environmental industry, we sometimes see some rather
curious arrangements. One of those curious arrangements is a
501c(3) non-profit organization, actually an umbrella organization,
called SEE, or Social and Environmental Entrepreneurs, Inc.

Social and Environmental Entrepreneurs, based in Malibu, California, states its purpose is environmental preservation, social jus-

tice, and education. SEE's 1998 income reported to IRS was $1,245,233 with assets of $337,720. By 2000, SEE's reported income is $1,711,981 with $615,923 in assets. SEE serves as fiscal agent for scores of "projects" which "work within SEE's umbrella", projects which benefit from SEE's fiscal management expertise and the use of its "non-profit" 501c(3) status.

SEE projects include Migrations/Black Mesa Weavers for Life and Land, and Northern Arizona Indigenous People's Defense Fund, formerly called Dineh Legal Defense Fund. Oddly enough, another SEE project is Public Lands Without Livestock, Director Mike Hudak, who is also associated with the national anti-grazing campaign. Hudak's writings are posted by RangeNet, a national networking organization at the center of the National Campaign to End Livestock Grazing on Public Land. Therein lies both SEE's hypocrisy and a curious insight into the machinery of the environmental industry, if one is willing to look.

As fiscal agent and umbrella for Northern AZ Indigenous People's Legal Defense Fund, SEE purportedly supports the Dineh traditionalists' fight against removal from their ancestral grazing lands, and their right to graze livestock on those traditional lands. All reservation lands are under the US Bureau of Land Management (BLM). SEE would also purport to affirm the Dineh's right to graze their sheep and cattle on these lands.

Yet SEE also helps the fight to remove livestock grazers from all "public" lands, which we all knew as federal lands before the environmental industry changed the lingo. The idea of this change in terminology is to engender a feeling of ownership and turn the urban public against livestock ranchers— to sign petitions, vote and campaign to demand removal of ranchers from federally managed land.

The national anti-grazing campaign's declaration calls "for a prompt end to public lands grazing" as an "essential first step" to "rewilding" the "western public lands". Hudak, just like his environmental industry colleagues, accuses livestock grazing of multiple high environmental crimes and characterizes public lands livestock grazers as virtually all 'big industry fat cats'.

In Ferry County, Washington, where I live, we have no big industrial livestock fat cats. We do, however, have many Indian and non-Indian family ranches, as is the case across the West. Hudak apparently doesn't concern himself too much with the many generational family ranches and incomes that will be lost if denied their traditional grazing allotments as he advocates. He merely states, with no hint of regret, that these ranchers are "waging a losing battle to remain economically viable". Nor does he bother to mention that many of those ranchers are Indian families that also stand to lose their livelihoods and ranches. Most interestingly, Hudak hasn't written a word of support for the Dineh traditionalist's grazing rights that I have been able to find.

It looks like SEE may be just one more high dollar environmental business that uses Indian people like a mascot to appear concerned, but in reality, to achieve political or financial objectives without regard for the social harm they will cause. Yet this is the political-economic landscape in which rural agricultural communities must find a way to survive.

Many of the factors already discussed come together in bold relief in Nevada's ancient Western Shoshone territory, known as Newe Sogobia to Western Shoshone. In that rugged range country, Indian and non-Indian ranchers alike face perennial threats of fines, imprisonment and livestock confiscation from federal management agencies that are highly influenced by powerful political-economic forces and environmentalism itself.

Non-Indian Nevada cattlemen like Ben Colvin, Cliff Gardner and David Holmgren face the same oppressive policies and threats to their livelihoods that Western Shoshone livestock ranchers contend with from year to year. Even elderly Indian people are not spared, as the BLM's continued harassment of Mary and Carrie Dann, as well as Western Shoshone National Council chief, Raymond Yowell, a member of the TeMoak Livestock Association, clearly illustrates.

At the center of the Nevada controversy is the 1863 Treaty of Ruby Valley between the Western Shoshone and the federal government. The tribe ceded no land in the treaty, but agreed to peace and friendship with the US. Under this peace and friendship treaty, the tribe agreed to accommodate new settlers on their land, agreeing to become "agriculturalists and herdsmen". The US government agreed to establish reservations sufficient for that purpose. However, like so many of its treaties with Indian people, the federal government did not honor its promises. The tiny little reservations it established from the tribes' vast landholdings in the early 1900's did not include nearly enough land for agriculture and livestock grazing, as promised.

Today, even though the federal government cannot produce documentation to prove how it acquired title to Western Shoshone lands, it now claims them. It says that the tribe has no right to them, despite their continuous occupation and use of the lands for over 10,000 years. The US government essentially sold these lands to itself 'for the Shoshone'. Thus the Western Shoshone struggle to resist having "payment" for their lands forced upon them, which would forever extinguish their rightful claim to their homelands.

In recent years, tribal appeals that show these lands were supposed to be part of their reservations have been put off by the BLM. A hearing scheduled for November 2000 was cancelled and never rescheduled. More recently, Nevada Senator Reid appears to be getting closer to success in forcing the tribe to take the payment. Raymond Yowell says, "We have always proceeded in a lawful and peaceful fashion. We have repeatedly requested the U.S. government demonstrate to us how they acquired our land. Under what law did they take our land? They have yet to provide an answer."

Yowell was among the Western Shoshone ranchers who lost their livestock to an armed BLM round-up on May 24, 2002. Before sunrise that day, armed BLM agents, with the assistance of several Nevada State officials, raided a tribal grazing allotment, seizing 136 head of cattle belonging to Western Shoshone ranchers.

Tribal members, members of other tribes, AIM members, local non-Indian ranchers, members of the Nevada Live Stock Association, members of the Nevada Committee for Full Statehood, and cowboy poet Waddie Mitchell all showed up to protest the

BLM's violation of Shoshone land rights and impoundment of their cattle. We should note that there was a conspicuous lack of any wealthy environmentalist supporters for the Shoshone ranchers, and certainly no activists in human-size bull trout get-ups.

Curiously, after that remarkable diverse display of support, a BLM official hinted that perhaps the Western Shoshone's tiny reservations might need to be enlarged. That is an interesting, if ironic and likely even ingenuous twist on the agency's stance that the claim has been extinguished, particularly in the face of Senator Reid's bill and the Yucca controversy.

BLM claims the seized cattle were trespassing on federal land because Yowell, like a number of other Elko county grazers, refuses to pay grazing fees to BLM to graze on Shoshone land. BLM bases its claim on a controversial Supreme Court case that ruled against Mary and Carrie Dann, in which the sisters attempted to assert the tribes' land rights. The court's ruling said the tribe has no judicial avenue to protect their land rights because the US Secretary of Interior accepted 26 million dollars 'on their behalf' as payment for their lands. Thus the federal government alleges that Shoshone title to over 24 million acres of ancestral territory has been extinguished. Catch 22, it is so because they say it is so.

Yet Western Shoshone say the Indian Claims Commission never considered the evidence that they still hold legal title to their land. A 1962 finding by the Commission says the tribe lost its land by a process of "gradual encroachment by white settlers and others". This notion defies the peace and friendship terms of the 1863 treaty in which the tribe agreed to accommodate settlers.

Western Shoshone maintain they were denied due process and the right to self identification and self representation. Their complaint has gone from US courts to the Organization of American State's Inter-American Commission on Human Rights, and the UN Committee on the Elimination of Racial Discrimination. The OAS Commission sent a confidential report to the US State Department stating the Shoshone's human rights were violated.

Western Shoshone Defense Council reports that documents released by BLM reveal the commission's report named the tribes' rights to property and due process as human rights that had been violated. On the local level, in addition to Western Shoshone claims, the Nevada Livestock Association and the Nevada Committee for Full Statehood also maintain that the tribes' right to due process and property rights were violated.

Apparently the Nevada state government and US Senator Harry Reid don't agree. Attorney General Frankie Sue Del Papa sent a letter to Reid that showed the State is not in favor of any legislation recognizing Shoshone land rights. Yet under Shoshone management of their lands, private landowners would remain and the land would be managed for the benefit of all the grazing communities and wildlife that depend on it. It is rather ironic that the state rejects the very land claim that would give it greater clout to resist the Yucca Mountain nuclear waste site it claims to oppose. Aside from environmental industry interests that never like to see the people's land leave federal hands, there are plenty of other competing industry interests for the vast Nevada landscape, Yucca Mountain nuclear waste proposal included. Reid's controversial bill to force payment and extinguishment of title on the tribe was created with neither the consent nor even the participation of any Western Shoshone tribal councils. It does not even provide for an adequate land base for the tribes' agricultural livelihoods nor any protection of the treaty.

Western Shoshone Defense Council reports the senator had never actually even visited a Shoshone community to explain his bill. This is the kind of faceless treatment Indian people, and now non-Indian people of the land, too, get today from so many politicians, federal land and water management agencies and, sometimes, even the state governments and national associations that once represented them. Add to that the pressures of the global marketplace and continually accelerating campaigns for alleged environmental purposes, and the outlook has been quite bleak for family ranching communities.

Ranching proponents additionally assert that the federal government's claim to ownership of 87% of Nevada land is a violation of the 1848 Treaty of Guadaloupe Hildalgo. Before Ne-

vada came into the Union, or even became a territory, the
Northeast's dominant old political-economic interests made their
attitude clear. They intended that they, not the actual inhabitants
of the land, would control Nevada's vast natural resources, especially its mineral deposits. It would not serve the interests of these
powerful monopolists for the land to belong either to the Western
Shoshone, the state of Nevada, or its non-Indian settlers. Federal
ownership, however, due to their influence in Washington, DC,
would preserve their hegemony. Thus some refer to Nevada as a
'permanent colony'.

Over the years, Indian and non-Indian alike, Nevada ranchers
have been threatened, jailed, fined and had their cattle rustled and
sold by the federal government. But the conflicts between federal agencies and Elko County communities are not limited strictly
to matters pertaining to cattle. Back in 2000, then TeMoak Western Shoshone chairman, Elwood Mose, a staunch supporter of the
tribe's treaty rights, was an officer of the Jarbidge Shovel Brigade, along with non-Indian neighbors.

The shovel brigade and supporters opened an access road the
Forest Service had closed purportedly for bull trout, a road that is
vital to the local community's welfare. Western Shoshone granted
the people access in the 1863 treaty, and the tribe maintains that
agreement is still in force. Hundreds of supporters from other
federally oppressed rural communities across the US converged
in Elko County to help the shovel brigade move – by hand – a car-
sized boulder that blocked the road. At that event, Mose told rural
people in general that they are the "new Indians", facing today's
threats and encroachments on rural communities.

On the creation of the National Forests, in *Storm Over Rangelands*, Wayne Hage shows that the Eastern establishment in the
late 1800's began to pump money into the new preservation branch
of the conservation movement to benefit their own monopolistic
intent. Eastern elite figures like George Vanderbilt and Teddy
Roosevelt themselves owned huge Western cattle and mining operations. Even then the elite's interest in conservation served
their own financial purposes.

What is today called the Forest Reserve Act of 1891 originally contained nothing about forest reserves. Section 24 that enabled establishment of such reserves was added as a last minute rider to a bill repealing the Timber Culture Act of 1873. Since this provision was not referred back to the originating Public Lands Committees of the House or Senate as required, the bill's passage was procedurally illegal.

Hage writes, "The bill went directly to a floor vote, and nearly every commentator says that Congress passed this most important bill without being aware of its content." Within sixteen years, Presidents Harrison, Cleveland and Roosevelt had already used the bill to exclude rural Westerners from over 37 million acres. Roosevelt's 1907 overnight declaration of 21 national forests in six Western states totaling 17 million acres - just hours before measures were enacted to prevent such actions without consent of Congress - sent shock waves across the rural West.

Jeffrey Mullens, associate editor for Knox News, reported when Yowell's cattle were herded up, confiscated and hauled off by armed BLM agents and Utah-licensed contract haulers. "O.Q. 'Chris' Johnson, speaking as chairman of the statehood committee, said his group can prove that the federal government does not own the land in question, and the only authority federal agents have is what county officials allow them. 'I think we need a change in law enforcement personnel in Elko County,' Johnson said, explaining that failure to support property rights in the Te-Moak case leaves the county vulnerable to other federal abuses."

David Holmgren, of the Nevada Committee for Full Statehood and third party gubernatorial hopeful, dressed as King George at the March federal trial in Reno of rancher, Cliff Gardner. Gardner, a neighbor of Yowell, ranches in Ruby Valley east of Elko. Gardner was convicted of trespassing his cattle on national forest land. He served one month incarceration at a halfway house and the last of three months of house arrest at his ranch. Gardner intends to appeal to the U.S. Supreme Court.

In August of 1992, a wildfire raged across Ruby Valley range land, stopping just short of Cliff and Bertha Gardner's home be-

fore coming under control. The size and intensity of the 1992 fire
was due to heavy rain and snow that produced an abundance of
vegetation which turned into volatile fuels for wildfire because the
Forest Service designated the range exempt from grazing that
year, saying the land needed a year of rest. Hundreds of thousands of taxpayer dollars were wasted fighting a fire that could
have been prevented by grazing the unusually lush growth to fire-
safe levels before it became dry enough to ignite the whole coun-
tryside.

But Forest Service officials admitted no wrong. Instead they re-
seeded the area and informed Gardner that the land then needed
two more years of rest from grazing. The Gardner's complied
with the federal agency in 1993, but by 1994 the situation had
again become a fire danger. The land around their Dawley Creek
Ranch was again growing thick with vegetation that left ungrazed,
the dry Nevada summer heat would turn into dangerous range-
land wildfire fuel, ready for the common dry lightning of the arid
West to ignite. The Gardners requested that the Forest Service
investigate the situation and allow them to graze the areas adjacent to their home and outbuildings to prevent destruction from
wildfire.

However, the Forest Service seemed only concerned with their
notion that land must be rested for two years after a fire. No one
was sent to investigate the fire danger Gardners warned of. Their
request to graze the fuel-like vegetation to safe levels were denied even though Forest Service regulations allow temporary grazing permits to use unusually abundant forage created by favorable
weather conditions. The Gardners decided that if the Forest Service was not concerned with protecting their home and family,
they would have to do it themselves.

On May 14, 1994, Cliff and Bertha sent a letter to the Forest
Service notifying them that they intended to graze the dangerous
fuels to safe levels. On May 19, the Forest Service officially
came to observe the Gardner's cattle grazing on the land. A day
or two later, they received a hand delivered letter from the agency
stating their cattle had to be removed by May 22nd. On June 9th,
the Forest Service cancelled Gardner's grazing permit and informed

them that they could appeal the decision. But Cliff and Bertha by then decided that the only way to get justice was to get the Forest Service out of Nevada, and challenge the federal government's claim to 87% of the land within its borders. Thus began Cliff Gardner's conflict with oppressive federal land managers.

Before the Yowell cattle impoundment, a March 27th Las Vegas Tribune editorial reported on the activities in Elko County. "A network is being formed amongst Nevada ranchers and Indians to monitor BLM movements within their counties and to sound the alarm if any impoundment actions are observed. The Western Shoshone have a 'minute man' system in place that reaches over treaty lands.

The Nevada Live Stock Association is implementing a first and second responder program of individuals who will come to the impound site as soon as notified. Immediate notification to both local and statewide press of any BLM or other agency menacing movements and actions against private property will also be relayed. Jackie Holmgren, Secretary for the Nevada Live Stock Association said, 'We shouldn't be afraid of taking such response. These are legitimate methods of sounding our displeasure with how these agencies are abusing our constitutional rights and have reversed the intent of the Taylor Grazing Act.'"

On March 21, David Holmgren sent out an alert from the Nevada Live Stock Association about Yowell's concerns over unusual BLM activity in his grazing area. Yowell said the BLM agents might be "trying to intimidate us by driving around all day. They may be looking to try and take our cattle right off of our checkerboard-deeded land and Indian trust lands."

Holmgren said, "I have alerted our directors, we are going to speak this week with Sheriff Harris of Elko County, we are speaking with Representatives from Jim Gibbon's office, and we have sent out a state-wide alert to be on the lookout for any suspicious BLM activities in the South Fork area as well as elsewhere in Nevada….Our policy is no more impoundment; due process and the right to property must be upheld. The press is being notified."

The alert also said the association received information from a source that wishes anonymity that, "The BLM has been dropping off horses by the semi-loads which they gather in one place and drop off in another, making money for their contractors and making themselves look like their doing something about the horse problem." The alert read: "The source believes that the BLM has been dropping off horses, 'on the Dann sisters or on the adjacent ranch now owned by a mine....The horses move over the ridge to the Danns. The Danns are then accused of overgrazing by the BLM.'" Yowell also said that a rancher from Roberts Mountain had proof that BLM was dumping horses on his grazing area. "Overnight, the horses showed up there."

The association said in the alert that it is looking into the allegations. Any evidence will be turned over to the sheriff or sheriffs, and the FBI. "This situation, if proven, leads us to the conclusion that the BLM is purposely creating problems for targeted ranchers," said Holmgren. The alert read, "The NVLSA in coordination with the South Fork Indian Reservation, other interested parties and elected officials will be present at the South Fork Reservation if any impoundment action is taken by BLM. The NVLSA is coordinating an impoundment contingency plan." It then gave directions to Yowell's land for supporters.

Perhaps the federal agencies' awareness of these cooperative arrangements between the Western Shoshone and non-Indian ranchers is why the Holmgrens received a threat to impound their cattle just before Yowell's were actually impounded. Some believe the Holmgren notice of impoundment in Mineral County may have been a diversion by federal personnel to make confiscation of the Te-Moak cattle in Elko County easier.

The majority of Western Shoshone people rejected federal payment for their treaty territory lands at a 1980 meeting of record, until such time that the federal government provides proof of ownership. Many Shoshone ranchers then began to refuse payment to the BLM, to protect their land claim. Under the pressure of the millions the federal government soon claimed was owed it in fines and fees, and the constant threat of their livelihoods – their livestock - being confiscated, the Duckwater and Yomba communities settled under protest. But ranchers at Odgers Ranch, the Dann Ranch and South Fork pressed on with their refusal.

So too, the non-Indian ranchers of Elko County and Nevada press on.

One might wonder where their efforts to cooperate will lead in these days of conflicting government promises and outside interests. Elwood Mose was replaced with a tribal chairman who soon called for a straw vote, similar to one years before on the land payment. Most tribal members did not participate in the vote in which the ballot itself was considered very misleading. Reportedly the only tribal members who favor taking their $20,000 share of the federal payment rather than their land are more or less urbanized members no longer living close to the land.

So the Western Shoshone still must persist in pursuit of their land rights, against great odds, as must the non-Indian ranchers of Nevada. As Iverson so aptly pointed out, they now face common threats, and a society that does not understand them.

That society is dangerously misinformed about the people who have lived so long in the rural landscape. It has rendered us a nation dangerously divided. The urbanized majority are persuaded by slick advertising, lawyers and lobbyists to believe that the people of the land are ruining the earth for them. They now believe they know a better use for the rural landscape than its inhabitants. This attitude is extended toward rural interior communities all the way to fishing and hunting communities that live with the sea. Meanwhile, the same old plutocratic elite benefit from the sacrifices that are demanded of the non-elite rural populace.

This is the second wave of Manifest Destiny, the enviro-economic re-colonization of the land. It will extinguish too many rural communities as their inhabitants have always known them, and as they want them to be, if those communities cannot determine their own futures.

This is what the inhabitants of the rural landscape face in America's new war over land rights, in this new era when everything from

industry and finance to environmentalism has gone global. The
rural life we know is vanishing. To those who experience it, it is a
very painful and socio-economically destructive vanishing indeed.
In this new American landscape, we will need each other to defend our human rights and freedoms in sufficient numbers. It is
only through that freedom that honest environmental responsibility can arise. We will have to cross party lines, find cooperative
resolutions to government's conflicting promises to us, and defend
our land-based communities - together - for future generations.

It is true. The proverbial fox is guarding the hen house. It's up to
us to chase him out.

-Chapter Ten-

On the Horizon

How can we move toward a just end to America's new war over land rights? How can we untangle government's conflicting web of promises to Indian and non-Indian communities? How are we to resolve conflicts between these promises and the promises government now makes for protection of the environment?

Most importantly, how can we realistically guarantee the socio-economic security and self-determination of rural land-based cultures, protect the natural resources we all depend on, and reverse the destructive divisions that characterize America's new war over natural resource rights?

There is a world of difference between the actions government historically takes in the name of the greater public good, and actually protecting the rights of all its citizens, particularly the urban and rural landscapes' non-elite inhabitants.

It is important to remember that abuse and oppression of rural peoples by a dominant political-economic elite began far back in the history of human civilization. Since the birth of urban cultures thousands of years ago, the rise of the city-state and the early days of empire-building, rulers coveted the land's riches to enhance their own political power over the urbanized masses and competing rulers.

They oppressed the rural landscape's inhabitants in order to control the riches of the land. Many large and powerful civilizations did not even question slavery or the taking of captives for that purpose. Thus land-based cultures have long been tossed around like pawns in the elite's contests for superior wealth and power. It is an old pattern.

Out of the dismal Dark Ages, out of feudal Europe and Britain, arose a class of merchants and artisans seeking and eventually gaining greater control over their own lives. The rural class, granted only tenant status, or less, on what was surely once their own ancient tribal land, soon aspired to the increased self-determination that land ownership could bring them. While land ownership did arise for some rural non-elite, economic and religious oppression still plagued the general populace.

These conditions set the stage for a flood of eager immigrants when empire-building Europe "discovered" and colonized Indian America. That event, bloody and destructive as it was for the land's indigenous peoples, set the stage for what may be the most unique and important cultural exchange in the recent history of human government.

After beginning their conquest of Indian America, the colonists rebelled against their own oppressive king, and adopted an American Indian form of government upon gaining their freedom. The new American union modeled its blueprint for freedom and human rights, the US Constitution, on the Iroquois Constitution, also known as the Great Law of Peace. Thus the United States of America was born.

On September 16, 1987, the First Session of the 100th Congress included a resolution "to acknowledge the contribution of the Iroquois Confederation of Nations to the development of the United States Constitution."

Though the truth of this matter has its determined classicist, or even Euro-centric, detractors, the facts are well established. Professors Bruce E. Johansen, University of Nebraska at Omaha, and Donald A. Grinde, Jr., University of Vermont, co-authored *Exemplar of Liberty*, one of four books resulting from over twenty years of their research. In reply to one published debunker, Johansen wrote—

"We do not advocate that anyone ignore the Enlightenment, the Greeks, or the rest of our European heritage. We are adding an Iroquois role to the picture….Lefkowitz may wish to examine a speech by the Iroquois sachem Cannasatego, in 1744, in which he advises the colonists to form a union like that of the Iroquois. She also should note Franklin's publication of Cannasatego's admonition on his own press, his advocacy of an Iroquois-style government in 1751, and his application of this idea in his Albany Plan of 1754."

Johansen points out the fact that "Iroquois leaders were invited to witness debates over the Declaration of Independence in Philadelphia during 1776." Thomas Paine learned the Iroquois language so that he would not be hampered in his understanding of these matters by reliance on interpreters. Yet today people educated by TV and stereotypes don't realize that Indian America had very advanced forms of governance.

Certainly the nearby living example of an advanced, constitutional, representative government piqued the interest of the Founders in search of a workable alternative to the Crown's tyranny. The colonies and Eastern tribes had already had government-to-government diplomatic relations – and war as well – for over a hundred years. The Founders were quite familiar with Indian government from that perspective.

I highly recommend reading the Iroquois Constitution itself. English translations are easily located on a number of Internet sites. This will confirm that the Iroquois League already had a government that featured checks and balances, a Congress-like council, protected freedom of speech and privacy of personal property, and many other features of advanced government. This constitutional government was in place for at least several centuries before the Europeans ever arrived. What was very different from the US is that it was the women's duty to choose or remove office holders for the good of the people. Yet women finally did get the vote and begin to take a role in US government.

Despite the fact that the provisions therein have been violated by errant leaders, this US Constitution, based on the time-tested prin-

ciples of the Great Law, remains the best framework for freedom
and human dignity that a diverse collection of sovereign states
and nations might hope to achieve. It is quite unique in history,
birthed from both the collision and cooperation of two once distant
cultures. It provides a common ground, the means to correct old
injustices and prevent further injustice, if only we adhere faithfully
to it.

Faithful adherence to this Constitution, I suggest, is paramount to
justly ending America's new war over land rights because it protects both Indian treaty rights to property and non-Indian property
rights.

Being humans after all, neither the Iroquois nor the US have been
able to practice the Great Law's principles perfectly, but that is
the beauty of its principles—you can always return to them and
they still work. This form of government, this system of law, is
designed to prevent abuse of the people when it is adhered to.

According to Iroquois tradition, the law was given by the Peacemaker, who traveled and taught throughout the land in a distant
time when people were in dire need of correcting their course,
some committed grisly acts of domination over others, and people
needed protection from abuse. There are some remarkable simi-
larities in this story to that of the biblical Peacemaker who also
traveled throughout the troubled land in such a time.

Come to think of it, when watching the news, it looks like we are
at such a time again. And so, it is a good time to recheck our
adherence to those principles. That is the beauty of these Constitutional principles—we can return to them when we have strayed
away, and they still work. They were designed to keep the darker
manifestations of the human family from dominating the rest of
humanity.

The indigenous American and non-elite immigrant European land-
based peoples, who were thrust into conflict by the Old World
political-economic elite, may have had much more in common than
those same elite wanted them to see. Had the non-elite immigrants not been so propagandized against America's indigenous

people before they ever even arrived, our history might have turned-out quite differently. As it was, the incidents of captive whites wishing to remain with their Indian captors in the East were numerous, attesting not only to the quality of their life among the tribes, but perhaps even distant ancestral memories of the European's ancient tribal way of life.

In any case, perhaps it is time now that we begin to think of this country of ours as the United States and Indian Nations of America. This thinking reflects all the land's inhabitants, its rich history, and the sovereign nature - inherent and promised - of the indigenous nations and the relatively younger states within this union. State, after all, is really another term for nation. Technically, the US arose not as a nation, but a union of sovereign states.

It is time for non-Indian America to cease fearing Indian America's desire for self-determination, for sovereignty - and visa versa - because it is really what we all want and need. It is time for the inhabitants of America's landscape to support each other's right to self-determination. The framework our Constitution provides is designed to accommodate such a union of sovereign states and nations.

This shift in thinking and action, I suggest, is another vital step toward ending America's new war over land rights justly. Together we can achieve this. Divided we are heavily outnumbered and likely to incur greater collective losses over time. This is, for rural communities, the socio-economically destabilizing era of enviro-economic globalization. Our unity will make the difference between cultural survival on the land, or increasing structural poverty, social harm and dispossession.

Land-based communities concerned about their futures should be proactive about achieving the kind of unity that can carry them through this newest wave of plutocratic assault on land-based peoples. We have varying degrees of understanding of each other's cultures, needs and aspirations. However, we can identify the bridges that exist and reinforce them so that we can reach agreement on the difficult conflicts forced on us by government's overlapping promises.

We can patiently and honestly work out resolutions to those conflicts and then insist that government accept them. This approach will protect our land-based communities. Fighting each other and allowing the distant elite's self-serving solutions to then be forced on us will not.

We must expose the corrupted system that purports to save the planet by demanding fatal socioeconomic sacrifice from the non-elite, sacrifices from which the privileged continue to profit. We must identify their financial sources and stop putting money in their pockets. We must make them accountable to the law, and to the public.

The aim is certainly not to eliminate philanthropy, but the current state of affairs in the environmental industry clearly illustrates it needs much closer scrutiny. Given the impact of foundation grants on our lives, we need to compare their investment interests and partners' interests, with the impact of its environmental giving on those investment interests and their competition. It does more harm to the people of the land to accept gifts from the elite class that undermine our socioeconomic sovereignty than it would to press for our needs without their self-serving, strings-attached grantsmanship.

I suggest that at this time there really exists more common need and latent common ground between sincere advocates of treaty rights, property rights, family agriculture, small business, labor rights, human rights and environmental justice, than exists between any of these advocacy areas and the plutocratic environmental industry elite. Its adherence to wilderness doctrine makes it profoundly obvious the environmental mainstream has more in common with the anti-human biocentric extreme than with people who need a realistic means of living on the land.

Possibly the most difficult issue is mining policy. Good water, and healthy soil and animal life are extremely important to rural people. We need to resolve our mining conflicts with both respect for local sovereignty principles, and the honest recognition that we use mined products. We need to defuse old anger and fear surrounding these issues and make sure we are dealing with facts.

Folks who believe that all mining is just plain wrong should first eliminate the use of absolutely all mined products from their own lives before they expect the rest of us to follow their lead. Unless we all plan to stop using mined products or feel it is right that we do all our mining in poor, developing countries far from our sight, we need to pursue unbiased science, and differentiate between responsible and irresponsible companies and practices. Some people who use mined products have a Not-In-My-Back-Yard attitude and don't seem to realize how elitist that thinking is.

We need to deal with sacred lands issues both with cultural respect and scrupulous honesty if they are to be happily resolved. It is obviously just as important that indigenous sacred sites be respected just as much as churches, cathedrals and sites of historical significance. Indigenous people need to ensure this principle is not misappropriated by people who might use it for other purposes, which is just another form of disrespect. If people are allowed to abuse this principle, any respect gained from other cultures for protecting indigenous sacred sites will be lost.

Protecting sacred places on the land is not compatible with wilderness doctrine. One attempts to preserve a place of great spiritual meaning for humans to access for respectful spiritual purposes. The other seeks to virtually eliminate human access to vast expanses of land. Yet people outside the Indian culture do not necessarily know whether a site is sacred or not, or whether the aim is like the wilderness objective to keep people out. The land-based communities involved in such issues need to communicate clearly and respectfully with each other to avoid misunderstanding. It is the kind of issue where the communities involved need to be wary of intentionally divisive influences in order to resolve it justly.

Land claims in the East where the tribal recognition process moves along so slowly have been particularly difficult. There is a growing trend in the East, however, for tribal land claims to exclude private property owners who acquired that property in good faith, recognizing their needs as well as the tribe's. This trend should assure their neighbors that they merely wish to insure cultural survival rather than retake the entire continent. It is time that the great contributions – and great sacrifices – of Indian America to our unique and diverse society be sincerely honored, and proactively heal the damage those sacrifices incurred.

If we determine to find win-win solutions to our conflicts, we will have the motivation of providing a better world for future generations, and a greater strength in numbers to empower us.

The people on the land must insist on balance between government's promises to us, and our obligation to nature. Land-based communities must take charge of the science that guides the management of the lands on which their lives depend. We must empower ourselves to prove that local stewardship is superior, both socio-economically and environmentally, to the token input land-based communities now have under big government blanket policies. Insuring local natural resource sovereignty will help balance and restore the socioeconomic security the urban labor force has lost to foreign manufacturers.

In the case of overlapping government promises for natural resource rights, we must be absolutely assured the science that is used to distribute those resources is valid. We must not blindly accept the science financed and promoted by the enviro-economic elite. Only developing our own management science with the communities involved, in both the spirit of mutual stewardship and mutual survival, will guarantee its validity and the security of our communities. This is what will protect our natural resources for the people's current and future needs, rather than reserving them only for a privileged elite.

We should repel the things that keep us divided against our own best interests. We need to be flexible, to cross party lines and social circles to meet on common ground in the manner that best insures *our* socio-economic survival. The political lay of the land has changed and demands that we adapt realistically. We must defuse our fears of each other, and insist in one loud voice on sane natural resource policy in the 21st Century American landscape.

Throughout human history, the strength of the land and the people on the land is what determines the strength and endurance of civilizations. Civilizations that abuse the people of the land ultimately crumble under the weight of their own corruption. As people of the land, we have a choice before us. We can either be divided, weakened and watch our diverse civilization crumble under the weight of the privileged and corrupt, or we can unite to strengthen our land-based communities and thus mend the fabric of society to the people's benefit.

It is up to the actual inhabitants of the rural landscape to end America's new war over land rights, if we want it to end justly.

Appendix

Bibliography

Index

Appendix

TESTIMONY OF ELWOOD MOSE, CHAIRMAN, TE-MOAK TRIBE OF WESTERN SHOSHONE INDIANS OF NEVADA IN OPPOSITION TO S.958 BEFORE THE SENATE COMMITTEE ON INDIAN AFFAIRS, 21 MARCH 2002

> If it were done when 'tis done, then 'twere well
> It were done quickly
> > Shakespeare, *Macbeth*, Act I, Scene VII

There are points to consider in paying out $136 million in mixed principal and interest from three Western Shoshone Indian claims judgments as proposed in S.958: 1) it benefits one-quarter degree blood eligible persons, 2) hands $1.3 million to tribal bureaucrats, and 3) Indian spending will help the economy. But S.958 has ethical, technical, historic and political problems. It is top down legislation and treats Shoshone descendants unequally. Only two other Native American groups, the Sioux Nation and Hopi Tribe, have claims outstanding.

The majority of the funds proposed to be distributed, about $135 million, comes from an Indian Claims Commission judgment made in 1977 for the Western Shoshone Identifiable Group as represented by the Te-Moak Bands in litigation that began in 1951. 1.3 million and $37K come from U.S. Claims Court 1991 and 1995 judgments. Te-Moak, created in 1938 under the Interior Dep't., was an umbrella organization under which Shoshone were to organize. But Elko, Nevada was distant and Shoshone created three independent local tribes, Duckwater, Ely, and Yomba under the Indian Reorganization Act. When Te-Moak revised its constitution in 1982 to become the Te-Moak Tribe, it had only four constituent bands: Battle Mountain Colony, Elko Colony, the South Fork Reservation, and Wells Colony over which it exercises central governing authority.

211

The first problem with S.958 is ethical. The federal Bureau of Indian Affairs has been nabbed repeatedly cheating the Americans it oversees. The Cobell litigation over trust funds accounting and backdating tribal recognition papers are public examples. Routine BIA Indian abuses draw little attention. In March 1998, the ten-member Te-Moak Council authorized a committee of four council and two tribal members to look into claims and what the Tribe might do about important issues. Two councilmembers dropped out and the two remaining ignored the two tribal members and established a rogue private "steering committee" to deal personally with top BIA regional and national officials and Reid's staff to promote a judgment distribution only. The committee set a vote on distribution outside tribal law in May 1998 for which the BIA turned out in force. It was a mystery vote. No one knows or will admit to who voted. The ballot was Hobson's choice. It reduced complex years-old Shoshone issues to a yea vote for 100% distribution at one-quarter degree blood or a nay vote for no payment at all. In January 1999 the BIA assistant secretary, deputy commissioner, and area director claimed to know of no claims legislation even though the Phoenix office had sent formally in December 1998 a secret draft bill to the BIA Central office. Only in August 1999 did Te-Moak finally receive a draft bill copy. It withdrew a 1997 ¼ blood quantum, 100% distribution resolution to develop a comprehensive tribal claims position.

The second problem is technical. In 1980, the BIA identified beneficiaries of the ICC Identifiable Group judgment to be descendants of Western Shoshone ancestry as proved by census rolls and records. The BIA then realized that it had ignored P.L. 93-134, a 1973 law by which "not less than 20 per centum" of a judgment distribution was to be set aside for common tribal needs. In 1982, the BIA amended its 1980 research report to designate the four Shoshone tribes: the Ely Tribe at Ely, NV; the Duckwater Tribe at Duckwater, NV; the Te-Moak Bands; and the Yomba Tribe located south of Austin, NV as "tribal successors to the Western Shoshone entity of the period 1853 – 1872...and beneficiaries of part of (the) award. The remaining beneficiaries consist of all other persons of Western Shoshone ancestry in their individual capacity."

In 1992, in testimony on Rep. Barbara Vucanovich's H.R. 3897 distribution bill, the BIA said, "We also recommend that Congress specify the blood quantum of those eligible...A one fourth (1/4) blood quantum requirement would be appropriate..." Other than that statement, there is no record, no adoption of a one-quarter degree blood standard for a person of Shoshone ancestry to be eligible for distribution—a ¼ blood degree requirement would cut out of claims money payment the very people on whose behalf the Shoshone claims was pursued: the descendants of the Western Shoshone Identifiable Group. A 1990 bill, H.R. 3384, proposed distribution to Western Shoshone descendants who joined a judgment fund distribution association. House Interior Committee chairman Morris K. Udall killed it. Rep. George Miller killed H.R. 3897.

The third problem is historic and political. For the last 23 years Shoshone have nixed claims payment as a pittance for up to 70 million acres of traditional lands. Shoshone issues have been unresolved from the signing of the 1863 Ruby Valley Treaty through claims litigation begun in 1951 to negotiations and distribution attempts. Sen. Reid, who denounces DOE Yucca Mountain processes ignores the BIA trampling Shoshone citizens' rights and endorses its misrepresenting claims payment support. The federals didn't stop there. They manipulated Te-Moak government and Te-Moak CFR court for payment: my council that withdrew support for distribution fell to a coup d'etat orchestrated by Elko, NV BIA Eastern Nevada Field Office superintendent Paul Young. F. Woodside Wright, a BIA employee and lawyer, issued a trumped-up eviction order of my council carried out by BIA police (we are currently suing Interior Secretary Gayle Norton and Wright in federal district court). The BIA, BIA-installed henchman Felix Ike and his fellow conspirators—swaggering opportunists—now make up an "Indian Ring" pushing claims money distribution. Global Crossing and Enron ethics and acts pale next to the villainy of the BIA, a politicized nest of obsolete sinecure and slimy practices that has to be abolished.

—oOo—

Harry Reid wants claims payment rammed through and everyone
salutes—federal might is right. A "free" cash bonanza payday is a
bright lure to Shoshone who lack the political clout and money to
influence Congress otherwise. No GAO investigates. S.958 is like
pouring a cup of wine into a barrel of muck to improve the muck.
Indians are still herded in this constitutional republic by federal
will and no matter claims cash will stay second-class citizens living on virtually lawless reservation ghettos under institutionalized
19th Century racial policy, existing in a dysfunctional federally determined welfare culture of phony egalitarianism where BIA power
and money corrupts and the BIA wields power and spends funds
corruptly. Senator Reid and Senator Ensign's federal charity may
be laudable but it is the federal government that beggars Shoshone
in the first place. What Shoshone—Americans all—need is the
equality of law and to be free of the chokehold of numbing federal
administration and agency bigotry.

ELWOOD MOSE
21 Lee B Unit 9, Spring Creek, Nevada 89815
Tel. 775/744-4274 Fax 775/744-2398
e-mail: mosetemoke@rabbitbrush.com

Bibliography

Books

Richard C. Adams, *Legends of the Delaware Indians and Picture Writing*, Syracuse University Press, Syracuse, New York, 2000

Ron Arnold, *Undue Influence: Wealthy Foundations, Grant-Driven Environmental Groups, and Zealous Bureaucrats That Control Your Future*, Free Enterprise Press, Bellevue, Washington, 1999

Dee Alexander Brown, *Bury My Heart at Wounded Knee: An Indian History of the American West*, Henry Holt and Company, 1970

Ward Churchill, *Fantasies of the Master Race: Literature, Cinema, and the Colonization of American Indians*, City Lights Books, San Francisco, California, 1998

Luke Cole and Sheila Foster, *From the Ground Up: Environmental Racism and the Rise of the Environmental Justice Movement*, New York University Press, New York, New York, 2000

Vine Deloria, Jr., *Behind the Trail of Broken Treaties: An Indian Declaration of Independence*, University of Texas Press, Austin, Texas, 1985

Jared Diamond, *Guns, Germs, and Steel: The Fates of Human Societies*, W.W. Norton & Company, Inc., New York, New York, 1999

Mark Dowie, *American Foundations: An Investigative History*, The MIT Press, Cambridge, Massachusetts, 2001

Frederic A. Godcharles, *Daily Stories of Pennsylvania*, Published by the author, Milton, Pennsylvania, 1924

Wayne Hage, *Storm Over Rangelands*, Free Enterprise Press, Bellevue, Washington, 1994

Hitakonanu'laxk, *The Grandfathers Speak: Native American Folk Tales of the Lenape People*, Interlink Publishing Group, New York, New York, 1994

Malcolm L. Hunter, Jr., *Fundamentals of Conservation Biology*, Blackwell Science, Inc., Cambridge, Massachusetts, 1996

Peter Iverson, *When Indians Became Cowboys: Native Peoples and Cattle Ranching in the American West*, University of Oklahoma Press, Norman, Oklahoma, 1997

Bruce E. Johansen and Donald A. Grinde, Jr., *Exemplar of Liberty: Native America and the Evolution of Democracy (Native American Politics Series; No. 3)*, American Indian Studies Center, 1991

Bruce E. Johansen, *Forgotten Founders: Benjamin Franklin, the Iroquois, and the Rationale for the American Revolution*, Harvard Common Press, 1991

Bruce E. Johansen, *Forgotten Founders: How the American Indian Helped Shape Democracy*, Harvard Common Press, 1987

Clifford M. Lytle and Vine Deloria, Jr., *The Nations Within: The Past and Future of American Indian Sovereignty*, University of Texas Press, Austin, Texas, 1998

Waldemar Nielsen, *Inside American Philanthropy: The Drama of Donor-ship*, University of Oklahoma Press, Norman, Oklahoma, 1996

Paul A.W. Wallace, *Indians in Pennsylvania (Anthropological Series, Penn-sylvania Historical and Museum Commission, No 5)*, Second edition, Pennsylvania Historical Museum Commission, 2000

Clinton A, Westlager, *The Deleware Indians: A History*, Rutgers University Press, 1990

Peter Nobocov, *Native American Testimony: A Chronicle of Indian-White Relations from Prophecy to the Present, 1492-2000*, Penguin USA, 1999

Theodore Roosevelt, *Theodore Roosevelt: An Autobiography*, Macmillan Publishing, New York, New York, 1913

Brian Tokar, *Earth for Sale: Reclaiming Ecology in the Age of Corporate Greenwash*, South End Press, 1997

David E. Wilkins, *American Indian Sovereignty and the U.S. Supreme Court: The Masking of Justice*, University of Texas Press, Austin, Texas, 1997

David J. Wishart, *An Unspeakable Sadness*, University of Nebraska Press, Lincoln, Nebraska, 1997

Grace Steele Woodward, *The Cherokees*, University of Oklahoma Press, Norman, Oklahoma, 1963

Articles and Studies:

Jacob Adams, Statement on Arctic Slope Regional Corporation's position on ANWR drilling, June 1995

Rebecca L. Adamson, *Sovereignty and intellectual property rights*, Indian Country Today, March 2, 2002

Jonathan Adler, *Inside the Green Mafia: The Big Environmentalist Grantmakers*, Foundation Watch Vol. I No.9, Capital Research Center, October 1996

Associated Press, *BLM sells seized cattle; demonstrators threaten block-ade*, Las Vegas Sun, May 31, 2002

Associated Press, *Researchers Blame Klamath Problems on Racism*, Fox News, December 19, 2001

Jeff Barnard, AP, *Klamath Basin offer gets mixed reception: Farm groups applaud the compromise, but tribes and conservationists are disap-pointed*, Seattle Post-Intelligencer, March 19, 2002

David Barsamian, *Being Left: Activism On and Off the Reservation - David Barsamian interviews Winona LaDuke*, Z Magazine, 1998

Zoltan Grossman, *Linking the Native Movement for Sovereignty and the Environmental Movement*, Z Magazine, November 1995

David Holmgren, *BLM Prepares to Rustle More Cattle: Cowboys and Indians Say No*, Nevada Live Stock Association press release, March 21, 2002

Audrey Hudson, *Scientists planted hairs from lynx in 3rd forest*, The Washington Times, January 4, 2002

Lee Juillerat, *There are lessons to learn, Tribes say*, Herald and News, March 31, 2002

Tom Knudson, *Taxpayer dollars help fund many environmental groups*, Sacramento Bee, October 22, 2001

Thomas E. Luebben, Guest Columnist, *Sordid legacy of the Indian Claim Commission*, Indian Country Today, March 16, 2002

Michael Millstein, *Klamath solutions originate in basin*, The Oregonian, April 3, 2002

Jeffry Mullins, *BLM to auction Yowell's cattle*, Knox News, May 28, 2002

Interior Secretary Gale A. Norton, *Interior commits to a broad Klamath Basin solution*, published in Klamath Falls Herald and News, March 27, 2002

Mark Sappenfield, *Rural America's clout in Congress eroding fast*, The Christian Science Monitor, June 13, 2001

Robert Schlesinger, *Two tribes split on Alaskan oil plan*, Boston Globe, February 25, 2002

Kimberly A. Strassel, *Rural Cleansing*, Wall Street Journal, July 26, 2001

Courtney Thompson, *Klamath Tribes seeks part of forest, The Native American group wants 660,000 acres of the Winema National Forest to establish a homeland*, The Oregonian, December 14, 1999

David A. Yeagley, *Indian Sovereignty in America*, FrontPageMagazine, January 14, 2002

Mary Ann Zehr, *It's a Wide Spectrum*, Foundation News & Commentary, Council on Foundations, Inc., May/June 1997

Index

Three to Get Ready

Looking to the future? Then you'll need these three books as signposts for things to come. Three prescient looks at where things are going in the years ahead, from savvy authors in the know. Now get three far-seeing books for tomorrow at the price of two!

Rules for Corporate Warriors by Nick Nichols. Tired of seeing your employer cave in to the demands of every do-gooder shakedown that comes along? Here's something to put a little backbone in your boss: a guide to surviving and thriving in the face of attack group campaigns, written by one of the nation's foremost crisis managers!

Gun Rights Affirmed by Alan Gottlieb. The future of your gun rights rests with the federal courts and the Emerson case! A landmark ruling says the Second Amendment protects an individual right to keep and bear arms, not just a government power to raise militias! Powerful reading!

Goodbye Green by Glen A. Duncan. How extremists stole the environmental movement from middle America and killed it. If you give money to green groups, you're being robbed! Get to the root of their hidden agendas!

The P.C. Three

Clever! Tasteless! Thought-provoking! Hilarious! Down-right philosophical! The three outrageously crazy Politically Correct books of humor will make you smile, belly-laugh, and smirk! Each is a 180-page quality paperback, three for the price of two!

Politically Correct Guns by Alan Gottlieb. A take-no-prisoners sortie deep behind enemy lines among the gun control crowd, jabbing them with their own hypocrisy and stupid actions, written by a leader of the gun rights movement.

Politically Correct Environment by Ron Arnold and Alan Gottlieb, with cartoons by Chuck Asay. Two leaders of the Wise Use movement poke a whole lot of fun at stuffy, self-righteous eco-pests, with political cartoons by one of America's boldest newspaper cartoonists.

Politically Correct Hunting by Ken Jacobson. Of course, there's no such thing as politically correct hunting, so Ken Jacobson takes a romp through the cherished beliefs of animal rights activists while sharing his many years of real outdoor experience as a hunter and guide.

Three to Get Ready

Looking to the future? Then you'll need these three books as signposts for things to come. Three prescient looks at where things are going in the years ahead, from savvy authors in the know. Now get three far-seeing books for tomorrow at the price of two!

Rules for Corporate Warriors by Nick Nichols. Tired of seeing your employer cave in to the demands of every do-gooder shakedown that comes along? Here's something to put a little backbone in your boss: a guide to surviving and thriving in the face of attack group campaigns, written by one of the nation's foremost crisis managers!

Gun Rights Affirmed by Alan Gottlieb. The future of your gun rights rests with the federal courts and the Emerson case! A landmark ruling says the Second Amendment protects an individual right to keep and bear arms, not just a government power to raise militias! Powerful reading!

Goodbye Green by Glen A. Duncan. How extremists stole the environmental movement from middle America and killed it. If you give money to green groups, you're being robbed! Get to the root of their hidden agendas!

The P.C. Three

Clever! Tasteless! Thought-provoking! Hilarious! Downright philosophical! The three outrageously crazy Politically Correct books of humor will make you smile, belly-laugh, and smirk! Each is a 180-page quality paperback, three for the price of two!

Politically Correct Guns by Alan Gottlieb. A take-no-prisoners sortie deep behind enemy lines among the gun control crowd, jabbing them with their own hypocrisy and stupid actions, written by a leader of the gun rights movement.

Politically Correct Environment by Ron Arnold and Alan Gottlieb, with cartoons by Chuck Asay. Two leaders of the Wise Use movement poke a whole lot of fun at stuffy, self-righteous eco-pests, with political cartoons by one of America's boldest newspaper cartoonists.

Politically Correct Hunting by Ken Jacobson. Of course, there's no such thing as politically correct hunting, so Ken Jacobson takes a romp through the cherished beliefs of animal rights activists while sharing his many years of real outdoor experience as a hunter and guide.

Three to Get Ready

Looking to the future? Then you'll need these three books as signposts for things to come. Three prescient looks at where things are going in the years ahead, from savvy authors in the know. Now get three far-seeing books for tomorrow at the price of two!

Rules for Corporate Warriors by Nick Nichols. Tired of seeing your employer cave in to the demands of every do-gooder shakedown that comes along? Here's something to put a little backbone in your boss: a guide to surviving and thriving in the face of attack group campaigns, written by one of the nation's foremost crisis managers!

Gun Rights Affirmed by Alan Gottlieb. The future of your gun rights rests with the federal courts and the Emerson case! A landmark ruling says the Second Amendment protects an individual right to keep and bear arms, not just a government power to raise militias! Powerful reading!

Goodbye Green by Glen A. Duncan. How extremists stole the environmental movement from middle America and killed it. If you give money to green groups, you're being robbed! Get to the root of their hidden agendas!